# the

# KETO DIET

## COOKBOOK

## FOR BEGINNERS

# 550 Quick & Easy Ketogenic Recipes to Lose Weight, Lower Cholesterol & Reverse Diabetes

### BY

### BABARA SAULS

# Disclaimer

Please note, the information written in this book, are for educational and entertainment purposes only. Strenuous efforts have been made to provide accurate, up to date and reliable complete information in this book. All recommendations are made without guarantee on the part of the author and publisher. By reading this document, the reader agrees that under no circumstances are we responsible for any losses, direct or indirect, which are incurred as a result of the use of the information contained in this document, including but not limited to errors, omissions or inaccuracies.

# Table of Contents

# Introduction

When you eat fewer carbohydrates and increase your fat and protein intake, it will definitely have a positive impact on your health through improvements in your blood sugar and cholesterol levels and by a decrease in your body weight. Once you get on the keto lifestyle, things tend to become easier and you're likely to see some impressive results. Ketogenic diet will make a change in your life and enable you to become a healthier person who can enjoy a new and improved life.

A keto diet is a low-carb diet that has changed millions of lives. When you live the keto lifestyle, it will mesmerize you and make you feel like a brand-new person living a healthier life. The **"The Keto Diet Cookbook for Beginners"**, contains everything you need to know about the ketogenic diet.

However, when you lower your carb intake, your body is forced into ketosis stage. Keto is a natural process in which our food intake is low for an extended period of time. It is a natural process the body initiates to help us survive when food intake is low. Ketosis enables us continue to thrive, reduced hunger, improve mental focus and performance. While in ketosis, your body begins to produce ketones from the breaking down of fats in the liver.

These procedure enables your body to produce energy to fuel your body's demands. The ultimate goal behind adopting a keto diet, is to continuously force your body into the metabolic state of producing ketones. When you're on a higher carbohydrate diet, your body will use glycogen as its main source of energy.

The benefits of the Keto Diet on your body include:

- It leads to improved cholesterol due to improved triglyceride and cholesterol levels from arterial build-up in your body.

- It improves mental focus and energy as insulin spikes and crashes are minimized due to decrease in carbohydrate consumption.

- It improves the blood sugar in your body since insulin levels are kept lower.

- It increases in weight loss to enable you shed weight as the body is burning fat as its primary fuel source, and limiting carbohydrates tends to decrease overall caloric intake.

- Ketogenic diet decreases hunger due to satiety provided by fats and proteins as well as increased vegetable intake.

# What is Ketogenic Diet?

Ketogenic diet is a low carb, moderate protein, and high fat diet that places the body into a metabolic state known as ketosis. It is a completely low-carb diet, where the body turns fat into ketones for use as energy. This helps to increase fat burning, reduces hunger and more. Ketogenic diet helps to restricts carbohydrate and protein intake to the point where the body converts excess fat into ketones. These ketones produced help to serve as an alternative fuel source for most cells in the body, supplementing or replacing glucose as a critical fuel source.

A keto diet is a low carb diet, where the body produces ketones in the liver to be used as energy. It can be termed as many different names – ketogenic diet, low carb diet, low carb high fat (LCHF), etc. When you eat any food that is high in carbs, your body will produce glucose and insulin. A ketogenic diet decreases insulin levels – allowing the formation of ketones to be used as fuel.

Glucose is one of the easiest molecule produced in your body to convert and use as energy so that it will be chosen over any other source of energy.

Insulin is also produced to process the glucose in your bloodstream by taking it around the body. The glucose is used as a primary energy, your fats are not needed and are therefore stored in your body. When your body is in higher carbohydrate diet, the body will use glucose as the main source of energy. By reducing the intake of carbs, the body is induced into a state known as ketosis.

# Getting Started to The Ketogenic Lifestyle

There's no special requirements to start Ketogenic diet. The basic guidelines and checklist to start the diet readily available in this book. Getting started into the ketogenic lifestyle is simple: just dive in! Always ensure that you plan ahead before placing yourself on ketogenic diet. Just bear in mind that the dietary restrictions can be a little bit intense and complicated.

Make sure to plan ahead and prepare to aid your success. A ketogenic diet can be great for people who are overweight, diabetic or looking to improve their metabolic health. It will not be suitable for elite athletes or those wishing to add large amounts of muscle or weight.

And, as with any diet, it will only work if you are consistent and stick with it in the long-term. That being said, few things are as well proven in nutrition as the powerful health and weight loss benefits of a ketogenic diet. Ketogenic diet requires you to restrict the intake of carbs to about 50 grams a day, which is substantially low than in traditional diets. In order to fill the energy gap or remaining calorific requirements of your body, the keto diet requires you to consume mostly healthy fats (65-75%) and adequate protein (15-25%).

# Top 8 Benefits of a Ketogenic Diet

The benefits that come with being on keto ranges from weight loss and increased energy levels to therapeutic medical applications. Everyone can safely benefit from eating a low-carb, high-fat diet. Below, you'll find the benefits you can derive from a ketogenic diet.

## 1. Weight Loss

Ketogenic diet uses your body fat as an energy source. Low carb, high fat diets have been used for centuries by doctors when working with obese patients to treat obesity. On keto, your insulin levels drop drastically which transforms your body into a fat burning machine. Scientifically, the ketogenic diet has shown better results compared to low-fat and high-carb diets. Many people around the world has successfully use ketogenic diets in their quest for decreased body fat levels for weight loss.

## 2. Control Blood Sugar

Ketogenic diet lowers the blood sugar levels as a result of the type of foods you eat. Ketogenic diet is a more effective way to manage and prevent diabetes compared to low-calorie diets. If you're pre-diabetic or have Type II diabetes, you should dive into ketogenic diet. Lowered insulin levels allow an individual to control and lower, their blood sugar levels. This ability to utilize fat and ketones as fuel for your body mean a pre-diabetic or a type 2 diabetic, no longer has to worry about excess blood sugar levels and the need to source exogenous insulin. There are lots of readers that have had success with their blood sugar control on keto.

## 3. Mental Focus

Ketogenic diets improve the brain function, clarity of thought, memory recall and improved learning. Lots of people use the ketogenic diet for the increased mental performance. Ketones serve as a great source of fuel for the brain. When you lower carb intake, you avoid big spikes in your blood sugar. This procedure can result in improved focus and concentration. Scientific studies have proved that an increased intake of fatty acids can have impacting benefits to our brain's function.

## 4. Increased Energy & Normalized Hunger

Ketogenic diet gives your body a better and more reliable energy. It will enable you to feel more energized during the day. Fats are one of the most effective molecule to burn as fuel. Fats are naturally more satisfying and ends up leaving us in a satiated ("full") state for a longer period of time.

## 5. Epilepsy

The ketogenic diet has long been successfully used to treat those suffering from epilepsy. Ketogenic diet was first developed in 1921 to treat drug resistant epilepsy in children. Hitherto, numerous studies have been carried out to show how ketosis can help with epilepsy. Epileptic children have continued to be seizure free long after they stopped their ketogenic trials. It is one of the most widely used therapies for children who have uncontrolled epilepsy today. The major benefits of the ketogenic diet and epilepsy is that it enables fewer medications to be used while still offering excellent control.

## 6. Cholesterol & Blood Pressure

The ketogenic diet helps to improve the triglyceride levels and cholesterol levels that is associated with arterial build-up. The low-carb, high-fat diets shows a dramatic increase in HDL and decrease in LDL particle concentration when compared to low-fat diets.

Scientists that has conducted research and studies on low-carb diets also show better improvement in blood pressure over other diets. The blood pressure issues are associated with excess weight, which is a bonus since keto has proved to lead to weight loss.

## 7. Insulin Resistance

Studies has proved that insulin resistance can lead to type II diabetes if left unmanaged. The research further shows that a low carb, ketogenic diet can help people lower their insulin levels to healthy ranges. An athlete, can also benefit from insulin optimization on keto through eating foods high in omega-3 fatty acids.

## 8. Acne

There are lots of evidence that ketosis can help clear acne. Studies has shown that high glycemic foods can stimulate acne outbreaks and as the ketogenic diet goes without such foods, it makes it easier to improve acne. Ketogenic diets help in the improvements of your skin when you switch to a keto diet. There are lots of studies that shows drops in lesions and skin inflammation when switching to a keto diet.

# What Do I Eat on a Keto Diet?

To begin a keto diet, you will need to plan ahead. It simply implies having a viable diet plan ready and waiting. The foods you desire to eat depends on how fast you want to get into a ketogenic state. The more you restrict carbohydrate intake, the faster you will enter into the ketosis state.

You will totally need to keep your carbohydrates limited, coming mostly from vegetables, nuts, and dairy. You should quit eating any refined carbohydrates such as wheat (bread, pasta, cereals), starch (potatoes, beans, legumes) or fruit. The exceptions you can eat are avocado, star fruit, and berries which can be consumed in moderation.

Always remember that keto is high in fat, moderate in protein, and very low in carbohydrates. Your nutrient intake should range around 70% fats, 25% protein, and 5% carbohydrate.

# Foods to Eat
## Majority of your meals should be based around these foods:

1. **Meat:** Ham, red meat, steak, lamb, beef, sausage, bacon, chicken and turkey.

2. **Fatty fish:** Salmon, trout, tuna and mackerel.

3. **Eggs:** Always eat pastured or omega-3 whole eggs.

4. **Butter and cream:** Look for grass-fed when possible.

5. **Cheese:** Look for unprocessed cheese such as cheddar, goat, cream, blue or mozzarella.

6. **Nuts and seeds:** Such as almonds, walnuts, sunflower seeds, flaxseeds, pumpkin seeds, chia seeds, etc.

7. **High Fat Dairy:** Such as hard cheeses, high fat cream, butter, etc.

8. **Healthy oils:** Such as primarily extra virgin olive oil, coconut oil, high-fat salad dressing, saturated fats and avocado oil.

9. **Avocados and berries:** raspberries, blackberries, and other low glycemic impact berries, whole avocados or freshly made guacamole.

10. **Low-carb veggies:** Such as green veggies, spinach, kale, tomatoes, onions, peppers, etc.

11. **Above ground vegetables:** Such as broccoli, cauliflower, etc.

12. **Sweeteners:** Such as stevia, erythritol, monk fruit, and other low-carb sweeteners.

13. **Condiments:** Look for salt, pepper and various healthy herbs and spices.

# How to Know if You're in Ketosis

You can assess if you're in ketosis through urine or blood strips. The urine strips are usually regarded as been inaccurate. Here's a list of some physical "symptoms" that usually let you know if you're on ketosis:

1. **Increased Urination:** Keto is a natural diuretic, so you urinate more often when you are in ketosis. Acetoacetate, which is a ketone body, is also excreted in urination. Ketosis can lead to frequent bathroom visits for beginners.

2. **Dry Mouth:** The result of increased urination can lead to dry mouth and increased thirst. Always ensure that you eat more salt and drink more water to alleviate these symptoms.

3. **Bad Breath:** Acetone is a ketone body that usually excretes in breath when you have reached ketosis. It may smell sharp like over ripe fruit that is similar to nail polish remover. The bad breath can range from being a little sweet to being almost like you've had a drink of alcohol. But the breath is always temporary and goes away long term.

4. **Reduced Hunger & Increased Energy:** You will notice a much longer hunger level and energized mental state when you get past the "keto flu," stage. It will result in less appetite which can allow you to go for hours without eating and don't feel very hungry.

5. **Add exercise:** Exercise is necessary to keep the body healthy. If you want to get the most out of your ketogenic diet, start doing exercise on daily basis for about 20-30 minutes. A 10 minutes' walk on daily basis can help regulate weight loss and blood sugar levels.

6. **Start supplementing:** Start adding supplements to help with a ketogenic diet. Although, the supplements are not usually necessary.

# Ketogenic Diet FAQs – Frequently Asked Questions

Here are some frequently asked questions about ketogenic diet and relevant answers to the questions.

### 1. Can I ever eat carbs again?

Yes, you can definitely eat carbs again. It is important to eliminate carbs initially. After the first 2–3 months, you can eat carbs on special occasions and return back to the diet immediately after.

### 2. Will I lose muscle?

There is a low risk of losing some muscle on any diet. But the high intake of protein and high ketone levels will help minimize muscle loss, especially if you lift weights.

### 3. Can you build muscle on a ketogenic diet?

Yes, you can build your muscles on a ketogenic diet. But it may not work as well as on a moderate-carb diet. However, keto diet helps to improve exercise performance.

### 4. Do I need to refeed or carb load?

No. However, a few higher-calorie days may be beneficial to your body.

### 5. How much protein can I eat?

Your protein intake should be moderate, because a very high intake of protein can spike insulin levels and lower ketones. The upper limit is around 35% of total calorie intake.

### 6. What if I am constantly tired, weak or fatigued?

These can only result when you are not in full ketosis or be utilizing fats and ketones efficiently. To remedy this, lower your carb intake. A supplement like MCT oil or ketones may also help.

### 7. My urine smells fruity? Why is this?

There's no cause for alarm. It is caused due to the excretion of by-products created during ketosis.

### 8. My breath smells. What can I do?

Bad breath is a common side effect. Try drinking a lot of naturally flavored water or chewing sugar-free gum.

### 9. I heard ketosis was extremely dangerous. Is this true?

Most people often confuse ketosis with ketoacidosis. But ketosis is natural, while ketoacidosis only occurs in uncontrolled diabetes.

Ketoacidosis is dangerous, but the ketosis on a ketogenic diet is perfectly normal and healthy for living the ketogenic lifestyle.

### 10. **I have digestion issues and diarrhea. What can I do?**

Most people on keto diet has this common side effect. It usually passes after about 3–4 weeks. But if it persists, try eating more high-fibre veggies. Magnesium supplements can also help with constipation and remedy the situation.

## Abbreviations

- tsp. = teaspoon
- tbsp. = tablespoon
- lb. = pound
- lbs.= pounds
- c = cup
- oz = ounce
- ml = millilitre
- kg = kilogram
- g = gram
- fl. oz = fluid ounce
- pt. = pint
- qt = quart
- gal = gallon
- L = litre

# CHAPTER 1: POULTRY RECIPES

## Lemon pepper roast chicken

Preparation time: 10 minutes

Cooking time: 1 hour 45 minutes

Total time: 1 hour 55 minutes

Serves: 6 servings

### Cooking Ingredients:

- 1 whole chicken, remove giblets
- 2 lemons
- ½ cup of ghee
- 2 sprigs of thyme
- Salt and pepper

### Cooking Instructions:

1. Start by preheating the oven to 350°F (175°C).

2. Wash with cold running water and pat dry the chicken. Place into a large roasting pan.

3. Zest 1 of the lemons, and rub the zest over the outside of the chicken. Season the chicken with plenty of salt and pepper.

4. Add the lemons, 2 sprigs of thyme and ¼ cup of ghee inside the chicken (stuff the inside of the chicken). Then rub the rest of the ghee on the body of the chicken.

5. Neatly slice the rest of the lemons and place them around the chicken in the roasting pan. Leave to roast in the oven for 85-125 minutes.

6. Check the temperature of the chicken by inserting a thermometer into the thickest part of the thigh and check the temperature is 165°F (74°C).

7. Remove from oven and cover with aluminum foil and rest for 10 minutes before slicing.

8. Serve and enjoy.

# Chicken & mushrooms

Preparation time: 5 minutes

Cooking time: 30 minutes

Total time: 35 minutes

Serves: 4 serves

**Cooking Ingredients:**

- ¼ cup butter (ghee for whole 30)
- 2 cups mushrooms, sliced
- Four large chicken thighs
- ½ teaspoon of onion powder
- ½ teaspoon of garlic powder
- 1 teaspoon of kosher salt
- ¼ teaspoon of black pepper
- ½ cup water
- 1 teaspoon of Dijon mustard (alcohol free mustard for whole 30)
- 1 tablespoon of Summer savoury or fresh tarragon, chopped

**Cooking Instructions:**

1. Start with seasoning the chicken thighs with pepper, onions powder, salt, and garlic powder.

2. Melt 1 tablespoon of the butter in a heavy bottomed sauté pan (preferably cast iron).

3. Sear the chicken thighs on both sides for about 3 to 4 minutes per side until golden brown. Remove the chicken thighs from the pan and set aside.

4. Then add the remaining 3 tablespoons of butter to the pan and melt. Add the mushrooms to the pan and cook for about 5 minutes stirring as little as possible.

5. Add the water and Dijon mustard to the pan, and give a nice stir to deglaze. Then add the chicken thighs back to the pan, skin side up.

6. Cover the pan and simmer for 15 minutes until the chicken is cooked through.

7. Stir in the fresh herbs and leave it for 5 minutes before serving. Serve hot.

# Baked Garlic Mushroom Chicken

Serves: 4 people

Preparation time: 15 minutes

Cooking time: 20 minutes

Total time: 35 minutes

## Cooking Ingredients:

- 1½ pounds chicken thighs, skin removed
- 8 ounces of mushrooms (white or cremini), sliced
- 1 cup chicken broth or bone broth
- 8-10 large garlic cloves, peeled and smashed
- 2 tablespoons of ghee
- ¼ tsp. onion powder
- ¼ tsp. ground dried sage
- ⅛ tsp. cayenne pepper
- ¼ tsp. black pepper
- ¼ tsp. salt

## Cooking Instructions:

1. Preheat oven to 375F. In a pan on high heat, add 1 table spoon of ghee and sear the chicken thighs for 2 or 3 minutes on each side.

2. Add the other 1 tablespoon of ghee and garlic in the same pan, and sauté for a minute or until fragrant.

3. Then add the sliced mushrooms and broth then stir and simmer for 1-2 minutes. Turn off heat and set aside.

4. Return the seared chicken thighs to the pan and make sure to distribute the mushrooms evenly around the chicken. Place the entire pan in the oven.

5. Bake it for 15 minutes or until the chicken is no longer pink inside. Separate the liquid, garlic and half of the mushrooms from the chicken to make the sauce.

6. Place it in a blender. Pulse until it turns into the consistency of gravy.

7. Serve and enjoy!

# Coconut chicken curry

Preparation time: 15 minutes

Cooking time: 45 minutes

Total time: 1 hour

Yield: 2 serves

## Cooking Ingredients:

- 3 chicken breasts, cut into chunks
- 1 tablespoon of ghee or butter or coconut oil
- 1 cup of coconut cream (skim from the top of 1 refrigerated can (13.5oz) of coconut milk)
- 1 cup of chicken broth or stock
- 2 cups of diced carrots
- 1 cup of chopped celery
- 2 tomatoes, diced
- 1½ tablespoon of curry powder or garam masala
- 1 tablespoon of grated ginger
- ¼ cup of cilantro, roughly chopped
- 6 cloves garlic, minced
- salt to taste

## Cooking Instructions:

1. Fry the chicken in the ghee, butter, or coconut oil in a medium-sized saucepan. Leave it to fry until the outside of the chicken has all turned white.

2. Add in the coconut cream and the chicken broth and mix well. Add in the diced carrots, chopped celery, and tomatoes.

3. Then add in the ginger and curry powder (or garam masala). Cook for 40 minutes on medium heat with the lid covered.

4. Then add in the minced garlic and cilantro and salt to taste.

5. Cook for another 5 minutes and serve.

# Crispy rosemary chicken drumsticks

Preparation time: 10 minutes

Cook time: 40 minutes

Total time: 50 minutes

Yield: Serves 4

**Cooking Ingredients:**

- 12 chicken drumsticks (with the skin on)
- 4 tbsp. (60 ml) of olive oil or avocado oil
- 4 tbsp. rosemary leaves, chopped
- 2 tbsp. (30 g) salt

**Cooking Instructions:**

1. Start by heating the oven to 450 F (230 C).

2. Rub salt on each chicken drumstick in the mixture and place them on a greased baking tray.

3. Drizzle the olive oil or avocado oil over the chicken drumsticks. Bake for about 35 to 40 minutes until the skin is crispy.

4. Serve and enjoy.

# Fried chicken

Preparation time: 15 minutes

Cooking time: 20 minutes

Total time: 35 minutes

Serves: 3 to 4 servings

**Cooking Ingredients:**

- 8 chicken pieces (wings, drumsticks with the skin on)
- 2 eggs, whisked
- 2 tbsp. (14 g) onion flakes
- 2 tbsp. (14 g) garlic flakes
- 2 tbsp. (16 g) nutritional yeast
- 2 tbsp. (14 g) crushed peppercorns
- 1 tsp. (1 g) Italian seasoning
- 1 tsp. (2 g) paprika powder
- 1 tsp. (2 g) chili powder (or to taste)
- 1 tsp. (5 g) salt
- ¼ – ½ cup (60 – 120 ml) coconut oil

**Cooking Instructions:**

1. Bread the ingredients by mixing the dry ingredients together.

2. Place the whisked eggs into a bowl. Add coconut oil to a small fryer and heat on high.

3. Add or dip each pieces of chicken into the egg mixture. Then cover with the breading and fry with the hot coconut oil.

4. Leave to fry for about 5-10 minutes depending on the size of the chicken pieces. Fry until chicken is cooked through and the outside is golden.

5. Do the same with the rest of the chicken pieces.

6. Serve with Keto Ranch Dressing or Keto ketchup.

# Chicken chili

Preparation time: 20 minutes

Cooking time: 60 minutes

Total time: 1 hour 20 minutes

Servings: 5 to 6 servings

**Cooking Ingredients:**

- ¼ cup (60 ml) of avocado oil, to cook with
- 2 oz. (900 g) of ground chicken
- 4 slices of bacon, diced
- 1 medium onion, diced
- 2 bell peppers, diced
- 10 white button mushrooms, chopped
- 3 chili peppers, seeds removed and finely diced (optional)
- 1 can (400 g) of diced tomatoes
- ½ can (85 g) of tomato paste
- 2 tbsp. (6 g) Italian seasoning
- 1 tsp. (2 g) chili powder (or to taste)
- 2 cloves of garlic, peeled and minced or finely diced
- 2 tbsp. (2 g) fresh cilantro, chopped
- Salt and pepper, to taste

**Cooking Instructions:**

1. Start by heating a large pot at medium high heat. Add the avocado oil.

2. Add the ground chicken, diced bacon, and diced onion. Leave it to fry until it turns brown. This should take about 5 to 6 minutes.

3. Then add the bell peppers, mushrooms, and optional chili peppers to the pot and fry for about 5 minutes. Season with salt and pepper, to taste.

4. Add the diced tomatoes, tomato paste, Italian seasoning, and chili powder to the pot. Cover and cook for about 50 minutes. Stir occasionally.

5. Remove the lid and add the garlic and fresh cilantro to the pot.

6. Cook for another 10 minutes. Cook uncovered. Season with additional salt and pepper, to taste.

7. Serve immediately and enjoy.

# Almond butter chicken sauté

Preparation Time: 1 hour (for marinade)

Cooking Time: 15 minutes

Total time: 1 hour 15 minutes

Serves: 4 people

**Cooking Ingredients:**

- ¼ cup (60 ml) of almond butter
- ½ chicken breasts, diced (or 4 boneless chicken thighs)
- 4 cups (60 ml) of olive oil
- 2 tablespoons (30 ml) of lime juice
- 1 tablespoon dried oregano
- Salt and pepper, to taste

**Cooking Instructions:**

1. Get ready the marinade ingredients and mix together (almond butter, olive oil, lime juice, oregano, salt and pepper).

2. Marinate the diced chicken for 1 hour. Remove the chicken and marinade into a frying pan on medium heat and cook until the chicken is cooked through and the outside is golden.

3. Serve with a salad and enjoy.

# Chicken adobo with cauliflower rice

Preparation time: 10 minutes

Cooking time: 20 minutes

Total time: 30 minutes

Servings: 3 to 4 servings

**Cooking Ingredients:**

**For the chicken adobo:**

- 4 chicken breasts, diced
- 1 onion, chopped into slices
- 3 cloves of garlic, minced or finely diced
- ½ cup (120 ml) of gluten-free tamari sauce or coconut aminos
- 1 teaspoon (5 ml) of apple cider vinegar
- ¼ cup (60 ml) of avocado oil, to cook with
- Salt and pepper, to taste

**For the cauliflower rice:**

- ½ head of cauliflower, processed into rice-like pieces
- ¼ cup of coconut oil (60 ml), to cook with

**Cooking Instructions:**

1. Preheat a large frying pan. Add the avocado oil into a large frying pan. Add the chopped chicken breast, onion, and garlic and fry.

2. Add in the tamari sauce and apple cider vinegar and place a lid on the pan. Cook for about 10 minutes. Scoop the sauce over the chicken periodically.

3. Fry the cauliflower pieces in the coconut oil to make the cauliflower rice, on high heat for 5 minutes until softened.

4. Serve the chicken adobo on top of the cauliflower rice. Enjoy.

# Chicken massaman curry with daikon radishes

Preparation time: 15 minutes

Cooking time: 25 minutes

Total time: 40 minutes

Servings: 4 serves

**Cooking Ingredients:**

- ½ onion, diced
- 2 chicken breasts, diced
- 3 tablespoons (45 ml) of coconut oil, to cook with
- 2 cups (480 ml) of coconut milk
- 3 tablespoons curry powder
- 1 tablespoon ginger, minced
- 1 tablespoon (15 ml) fish sauce
- ¼ cup (60 ml) of almond butter
- 2 tablespoons (30 ml) lime juice
- 1 Daikon radish (300 g), peeled and diced
- 2 tablespoons cilantro, chopped
- Salt and pepper, to taste

**Cooking Instructions:**

1. Add coconut oil to a large pan and leave it till it gets brown.

2. Add the chicken and leave to brown. Add coconut milk, curry powder, ginger, fish sauce, almond butter, daikon radishes, and lime juice and cook for about 15 minutes.

3. Add in cilantro and salt to taste.

4. Serve and enjoy.

# Spicy chicken casserole

Preparation time: 10 minutes

Cooking time: 75 minutes

Total time: 85 minutes

Serves: 7 to 8 servings

## Cooking Ingredients:

- 2 chicken breasts (400 g), diced
- 2 heads of broccoli (900 g), broken into small florets
- ½ red onion, diced
- 10 white button mushrooms, diced
- 12 slices of bacon, diced
- 2 chili peppers, de-seeded and diced (add more if you like it spicier)
- 2 cups of coconut cream (480 ml), to cover the dish
- 4 tablespoons of coconut oil (60 ml), to cook chicken in
- Salt and pepper, to taste

## Cooking Instructions:

1. Start by heating the oven to 350 F (175 C). Add the coconut oil to a frying pan and cook the diced bacon. Cook until it starts to get crispy.

2. Then add the diced chicken breast and cook through until it gets brown. Add salt and pepper to taste.

3. Then add everything to a large baking pan. Bake for 1 hour uncovered. Place the broccoli on the bottom of the pan so as to avoid them getting burned.

4. Serve and enjoy.

# Buffalo wings

Preparation time: 15 minutes

Cooking time: 45 minutes

Total time: 1 hour

Serves: 4 serves

**Cooking Ingredients:**

- 12 small chicken wings
- ½ cup of coconut flour
- ½ teaspoon of cayenne pepper
- ½ teaspoon of black pepper
- ½ teaspoon of crushed red pepper flakes
- 1 tablespoon of paprika
- 1 tablespoon of garlic powder
- 1 tablespoon of salt
- ¼ cup of ghee, melted
- ¼ cup of hot sauce

**Cooking Instructions:**

1. Heat the oven to 400F. Mix the dry ingredients (coconut flour, dried spices, and salt) together in a bowl.

2. Cover each chicken wing with the coconut flour mixture. Then refrigerate for about 15-30 minutes to help the flour stick on a bit better (it is optional).

3. Prepare a baking tray by lining it with aluminium floor or grease the tray. Then mix the ghee and the hot sauce together well.

4. Dip each chicken into the ghee and hot sauce mixture and place onto the baking tray and leave it to bake for 35 to 45 minutes.

5. Serve and enjoy.

# Chicken Cauliflower Mac and Cheese

Preparation time: 10 minutes

Cooking time: 37 minutes

Gross time: 47 minutes

## Cooking Ingredients:

- 1 cauliflower head, cut into florets
- 2 cups of chopped skinless rotisserie chicken
- 4 oz. cream cheese, cut into cubes
- ¼ teaspoon of sea salt
- 2 cups of Tillamook Farm style cut medium cheddar cheese, divided
- 1 teaspoon chopped parsley

## Cooking Instructions:

1. First heat the oven to about 400 degrees F.

2. Add the chopped chicken, cauliflower, and cream cheese to a cast iron skillet. Cover with foil and bake for 15 to 20 minutes.

3. Remove from oven. Add salt, 1½ cups cheese and parsley and stir. Cover it with foil and bake again for another 15 minutes.

4. Remove from oven and add the remaining ½ cup of cheese. Broil for 2 minutes.

5. Serve and enjoy.

# Macadamia Nut Chicken Thighs

Preparation time: 15 minutes

Cooking time: 30 minutes

Gross time: 45 minutes

Serves: 5 to 6 People

## Cooking Ingredients:

- 12 chicken thighs, boneless, skinless
- 3 large eggs
- ¼ cup of almond milk, unsweetened
- 2 cups macadamia nuts
- 1 cup of coconut flour, or all-purpose flour
- 1½ of teaspoons kosher salt
- ½ of teaspoon black pepper
- 4 tablespoons butter, melted
- US Customary - Metric

## Cooking Instructions:

1. Add 2 cups of macadamia nuts and 1 cup of coconut flour to a food processor and process until the mixture resembles coarse crumbs.

2. Put the nut mixture in a pan and season with 1 teaspoon of salt and ½ teaspoon of black pepper.

3. In a second shallow dish, whisk together the eggs, almond milk, ½ teaspoon salt, and ¼ teaspoon black pepper. Add the chicken thighs, 3 at a time, to the egg mixture. Coat both sides of the chicken.

4. Add the egg-coated thighs to the macadamia nut mixture. Press the crumbs onto each side of the chicken.

5. Spray baking dish with baking spray and place the chicken on it. Sprinkle any remaining nuts evenly over the chicken in the pan.

6. Preheat oven to 375-degree. Pour evenly melted butter on the macadamia coated chicken and bake for 25 to 30 minutes, or until the chicken juices run clear when pierced, or when the internal temperature reaches 165 degrees.

7. Serve and enjoy.

# Chicken Korma

Cooking time: 40 minutes

Preparation time: 10 minutes

Total time: 50 minutes

## Cooking Ingredients:

- ¼ cup of almond butter
- 3 cloves of garlic, peeled
- 1 (½ inch) piece fresh ginger root, peeled and chopped
- 2½ tablespoons ghee or butter
- ½ medium-sized onion, minced
- 1 teaspoon of ground coriander
- 1 teaspoon of garam masala
- 1 teaspoon of ground cumin
- 1 teaspoon of ground turmeric
- 1 teaspoon of chili powder
- 3 skinless, boneless chicken breast halves – diced
- 1/3 cup of tomato sauce
- 1/3 cup of chicken broth
- ½ cup of coconut milk
- ½ cup of unsweetened plain greek yogurt or unsweetened plain coconut milk yogurt for paleo

## Cooking Instructions:

1. Blend garlic and ginger until it gets smooth and set aside. Heat ghee or butter over medium heat.

2. Add onion, and cook until it softens. This should take about 3 to 5 minutes. Then add and mix the ginger and garlic paste.

3. Add coriander, garam masala, cumin, turmeric, and chili powder. Give a good stir until well combined.

4. Stir in diced chicken, and cook for about 5 minutes. Add the tomato sauce and chicken broth over chicken. Heat until broth starts bubbling.

5. Then cover the lid, reduce heat, and simmer for 15 minutes, stirring occasionally. Add the almond butter, coconut milk and yogurt in a food processor. Process until smooth.

6. Stir the almond butter coconut milk mixture into the chicken and sauce. Cover the lid and cook on low heat for 10 to 12 minutes, stirring occasionally. Serve immediately and enjoy.

# Chicken Florentine in a Skillet

Serves: 3 to 4 people

Preparation time: 5 minutes

Cooking time: 30 minutes

Gross time: 35 minutes

**Cooking Ingredients:**

- 4 chicken thighs (bone-in, skin-on)
- 2 tablespoons of avocado oil
- ¾ cups of chicken stock
- 1 cups of heavy whipping cream
- ½ teaspoon of pink Himalayan sea salt
- ¼ teaspoon of black pepper
- ½ teaspoon of Italian seasoning
- ½ teaspoon of onion powder
- ½ teaspoon of garlic powder
- 8 ounces of cremini mushrooms, sliced
- ¾ cups of shredded parmesan cheese
- 3 cups of spinach

**Cooking Instructions:**

1. Heat the avocado oil over medium high heat in a stainless-steel pan (or cast-iron skillet).

2. Add the chicken thighs and leave to cook for 6 to 8 minutes. Chicken should be well cooked.

3. After the chicken has been cooked, remove from the skillet and place it on a plate or tray.

4. Add your spices, heavy whipping cream and the chicken stock to the skillet.

5. Give a good stir. Once the mixture starts to simmer, reduce the heat to Low, then add mushrooms and leave it to cook till it softens.

6. Put the cups of spinach and Parmesan cheese. Give a thorough stir until the cheese is mixed and melted.

7. Cook the chicken in the skillet again for about 5 minutes and give stir simultaneously until the chicken is well cooked. Serve and enjoy.

# Shredded Chicken Chili

Preparation time: 5 minutes

Cooking time: 25 minutes

Gross time: 30 minutes

Serves: 5 to 6 people

## Cooking Ingredients:

- 4 chicken breasts large, shredded
- 1 tablespoon of Butter
- ½ onion chopped
- 2 cups of chicken broth
- 10 ounces of diced tomatoes canned, undrained
- 2 ounces of tomato paste
- 1 tablespoon of Chilli powder
- 1 tablespoon of Cumin
- ½ tablespoon of Garlic powder
- 1 jalapeno pepper chopped (optional)
- 4 ounces of Cream cheese
- Salt and pepper to taste

## Cooking Instructions:

1. Boil chicken breasts in water or broth on stovetop for 12 minutes until the meat is no longer pink. Remove the chicken from the liquid and shred with two forks.

2. Melt butter in a large stock pot at a medium-high heat. Add the chopped onions and cook.

3. Boil the shredded chicken, chicken broth, diced tomatoes, chili powder, tomato paste, garlic powder, chili powder and jalapeno in the pot.

4. Put it down in a simmer at medium-low heat and leave it covered for 8 to 10 minutes.

5. Cut cream cheese into small pieces. Remove lid and mix with the cream cheese. Place the heat at medium-high and give a good.

6. Bring it down from the heat, season with pepper and salt. Serve and enjoy.

# Chicken Parmesan

Preparation time: 5 minutes

Cooking time: 25 minutes

Total time: 30 minutes

Serves: 4 People

**Cooking Ingredients:**

- 4 chicken breasts
- 1 cup of passata
- 1 cup of shredded mozzarella.
- ½ cup of grated Parmigiano-Regiano or pecorino romano
- 3 tablespoons of olive oil. Extra virgin. You can add more if you're a big fan.
- 1 minced garlic clove
- 1 teaspoon dried oregano
- 1 teaspoon dried thyme
- 1 teaspoon smoked paprika for extra flavour
- salt & pepper to taste
- You can also use Italian Seasoning if you like

**Cooking Instructions:**

1. Preheat your oven to 400F. Add 1 table spoon of olive oil on a warmed-up skillet.

2. On high-heat, sear your chicken breasts for 4 minutes on each side. Until the colour changes.

3. Add your diced tomatoes and olive oil on a warmed up sauce pan. Add your finely chopped garlic to the sauce. Add Salt & Pepper to your taste.

4. Scoop one table spoon of sauce on top of each chicken cutlet, sprinkle some shredded cheese and your dried herbs.

5. Bake for 15 minutes. Take out and let it cool down for 10 minutes before serving. Enjoy.

# Cashew Chicken

Preparation time: 15 minutes

Cooking time: 10 minutes

Total time: 25 minutes

Serves: Serves 3

## Cooking Ingredients:

- 3 raw chicken thighs boneless, skinless
- 2 tablespoons of coconut oil (for cooking)
- ¼ cup raw cashews
- ½ medium Green Bell Pepper
- ½ teaspoon of ground ginger
- 1 tablespoon of rice wine vinegar
- 1½ tablespoon of liquid aminos
- ½ tablespoon of chili garlic sauce
- 1 tablespoon of minced garlic
- 1 tablespoon of Sesame Oil
- 1 tablespoon of Sesame Seeds
- 1 tablespoon of green onions
- ¼ medium white onion
- Salt + Pepper

## Cooking Instructions:

1. First heat a pan over low heat and toast the cashews for about 7 to 8 minutes or until they start to lightly brown and become fragrant.

2. Cut or chop onions and pepper in large chunks, dice chicken into 1-inch chunks. Increase the heat to high and add 2 tablespoon of coconut oil to pan.

3. Add the chicken thighs when the coconut oil is hot enough. Cook for about 5 to 6 minutes.

4. Add in the pepper, onions, garlic, chili garlic sauce and seasonings (ginger, salt, pepper) and leave to cook on high for 2 to 3 minutes.

5. Put rice wine vinegar, liquid aminos, and the cashews. Allow to cook for few minutes on high until the liquid reduces.

6. Serve immediately, top with sesame seeds and drizzle with sesame oil. Enjoy!

# Chicken and Mushroom Skillet in a Creamy Asiago and Mustard Sauce

Preparation time: 5 minutes

Cooking time: 25 minutes

Gross time: 30 minutes

Servings: 4 people

**Cooking Ingredients:**

- 2 tablespoons of oil or butter
- 4 (6 oz.) boneless skinless chicken breasts, pounded thin
- salt and pepper to taste
- 8 ounces of mushrooms, sliced
- 1 small onion, diced
- 2 cloves garlic, chopped
- 1 teaspoon of thyme, chopped
- ¼ cup dry white wine or chicken broth
- ½ cup chicken broth
- ½ cup heavy/whipping cream
- 1 tablespoon of grainy mustard
- 1 tablespoon of dijon mustard
- salt and pepper to taste
- ½ cup asiago cheese, grated

**Cooking Instructions:**

1.  Season the chicken with salt and pepper to your taste. Heat the oil in a heavy bottomed skillet over medium-high heat.

2.  Add the chicken to the pan and cook until golden brown on both sides, about 6 minutes per side.

3.  Cut the onions and cook them with the mushrooms until the mushrooms have released their liquid and it has evaporated (10 minutes).

4.  Add in the thyme and garlic and cook for 30 seconds. Add the wine and deglaze the pan.

5.  Mix the broth and cream, mix in the mustards. Add season with salt and pepper to taste.

6.  Add the chicken, bring to a boil and cook for about 5 minutes until the sauce thickens.

7.  Add the asiago and let it melt, remove from heat. Serve and enjoy!

# Cheesy Chicken Meatballs

Preparation time: 10 minutes

Cooking time: 30 minutes

Gross time: 40 minutes

Serves: 3 to 4 servings

**Cooking Ingredients:**

- 1-pound of ground chicken can sub ground turkey or beef
- 2 tbsp. of Minced Garlic
- ½ tsp. of Italian seasoning
- ½ cup of mozzarella cheese shredded
- ¼ cup of salt or sugar added marinara sauce
- 2 tbsp. of salt or sugar added marinara sauce for topping
- Salt to taste
- dried parsley for garnish

**Cooking Instructions:**

1. First heat the oven to 350 F. Prepare an 8x8" baking sheet. Place a thin layer of marinara sauce on the bottom.

2. Mix the ground chicken, garlic, Italian seasoning, salt, pepper and marinara sauce in a large bowl.

3. Roll the mixture into 12 meatballs and place them on the prepared baking sheet. Bake for 20 minutes at 350 F.

4. Remove from the oven then turn the oven to a low broil.

5. Place remaining marinara sauce on top of each meatball and cheese on top. Cook for 5 minutes until cheese is melted.

6. Serve with salad of spinach and bell pepper. Enjoy.

# Chicken Cordon Bleu

Preparation time: 10 minutes

Cooking time: 30 minutes

Total time: 40 minutes

Serves: 5 serves

## Cooking Ingredients:

- 5 pieces of chicken breast fillets about 750 grams
- ¾ c. cheese of choice freshly grated (I used Edam)
- 5 pieces round ham slices thinly cut
- 5 slices mozzarella 1/3-inch thick, placed in freezer for 1 hour
- 1 egg beaten
- ½ c. unsweetened shredded coconut
- ½ tsp. of ground sage
- ¾ tsp. of dried basil
- ¾ tsp. of dried marjoram
- salt & ground black pepper to taste

## Cooking Instructions:

1. Add and mix sage, basil and marjoram.

2. Wash chicken with cold water, pat dry. Make an incision with a knife at the side of chicken and slice without cutting in half.

3. Open chicken fillet and season with salt, black pepper and mixed herbs. Season evenly.

4. Lay 1 slice of ham, 1 tablespoon of grated cheese and top with frozen mozzarella cheese. Fold them and seal the edges with toothpick.

5. Add egg and 1/8 teaspoon of mixed herbs. Dip both sides of stuffed chicken fillet.

6. Spread dried shredded coconut and sprinkle the remaining mixed herbs on a plate. Then season with salt and pepper to taste. Coat stuffed chicken fillet.

7. Place the chicken fillet on a slightly greased baking pan with foil. Cover loosely with foil or paper.

8. Bake in a preheated oven at 400°F for 20 minutes. Remove foil and place in the broiler until coating is golden in colour.

9. Remove and transfer to a platter, serve with Cheese Sauce on the side. Enjoy!

# CHAPTER 2: PORK, BEEF & LAMB RECIPES

## Cheese Taco Shells

Serves: 4 people

Preparation time: 20 minutes

Cooking time: 10 minutes

Gross time: 30 minutes

### Cooking Ingredients:

- 2 cups of shredded Cheddar
- Freshly ground black pepper
- 1 tablespoon of vegetable oil
- 1 white onion, chopped
- 1 pound of ground beef
- 1 tablespoon of Taco Seasoning
- shredded lettuce, for serving
- Chopped tomatoes, for serving
- Hot sauce, for serving

### Cooking Instructions:

1. First heat the oven to 375°. Prepare a baking sheet with parchment paper and spray with cooking spray.

2. Add ½ cup mounds of cheddar on baking sheet and season with pepper. Bake for 5 to 7 minutes. Blot grease with a paper towel.

3. Set up 4 stations of two upside-down glasses and a wooden spoon as a bridge. Transfer cheese mounds to wooden spoons to form shell (use a spatula for this).

4. In a large skillet over medium heat, heat oil. Add onions and cook for 5 minutes until tender.

5. Then add ground beef and cook until no longer pink, 6 minutes more. Drain the fat and season with taco seasoning.

6. Assemble tacos: Place beef in shells and top with lettuce, tomatoes, and hot sauce.

7. Serve and enjoy.

# Cream Cheese Stuffed Meatballs

Preparation time: 15 minutes

Cooking time: 15 minutes

Gross time: 30 minutes

**Cooking Ingredients:**

**Meatballs:**

- 1 spring onion finely sliced
- 1 clove garlic crushed
- 750 g ground/mincemeat. I used pork
- salt and pepper to taste
- 1 egg slightly beaten
- 2 slices bacon finely chopped
- 3 tablespoons of sun-dried tomatoes finely diced
- 2 tablespoons of favourite herbs - I use rosemary, thyme, oregano and sage

**Filling:**

- 110 g cream cheese diced into squares

**Cooking Instructions:**

1. Add all your meatball ingredients on a large mixing bowl. Mix thoroughly with your hands.

2. Scoop up a golf ball size of meatball mixture (use a desert spoon). Squeeze the mixture into a ball then flatten into a circle.

3. Place a cube of cream cheese in the centre of the meatball circle then enclose the meatball mixture around the cream cheese.

4. On a greased baking tray, place the cream cheese stuffed meatball. Repeat until all the mixture has been used.

5. Spray them all with olive oil spray so they will crisp and brown beautifully.

6. Bake at 180C/350F for 15-20minutes depending on your oven.

7. Serve and enjoy.

# Taco Seasoning

Preparation time: 5 minutes

Cooking time: 10 minutes

Gross time: 15 minutes

## Cooking Ingredients:

- 1 tablespoon of ground chili powder
- 1½ teaspoons of ground cumin
- 1 teaspoon of paprika
- ½ teaspoon of granulated garlic
- ½ teaspoon of granulated onion
- ½ teaspoon of dried oregano, rubbed
- ½ teaspoon of salt
- ¼ teaspoon of pepper

## Optional:

- 1 teaspoon of Sukrin :1 (Swerve Granulated or sugar if not low carb)

## Cooking Instructions:

1. Measure and gather all of the ingredients into a small bowl and whisk with a fork. Keep them in an airtight container.

2. Serves 6-12 people depending on your taste. 1-carb per 2 teaspoons of seasoning or ½ carb per 1 teaspoon of seasoning.

3. Brown 1 pound of ground beef in a pan. Add 2 to 4 tablespoons (half of the recipe or the whole thing) to the ground beef along with 2 tablespoons of tomato paste and ½ cup beef broth.

4. Cook gently until most of the sauce evaporates. Adjust seasoning with salt and pepper.

5. Carb counts will depend on how much seasoning you use.

# Spicy Beef Ramen

Preparation time: 10 minutes

Cooking time: 20minutes

Total time: 30 minutes

Serves: 4 serves

## Cooking Ingredients:

- 1-pound 80/20 ground beef, browned and crumbled
- ½ small onion, diced
- 2 cloves minced garlic
- ¼ to ½ teaspoon ground ginger
- 2 tablespoons vegetable oil
- 1 teaspoon of sesame oil
- 2 cups of beef broth
- 2 tablespoons soy sauce
- 2 packages Miracle angel hair noodles
- ½ cup of green onions, chopped
- garnish: red pepper flakes
- Optional: Sriracha sauce for more heat. This is not factored in to the nutrition count. You would add 1.3-carbs per teaspoon added.

## Cooking Instructions:

1. Prepare the ground beef and set aside. In the same pan, fry the onion, garlic, ginger, vegetable, and sesame oil. Sauté over medium for several minutes.

2. Then add the beef broth and soy sauce and cook for a few minutes. Turn heat to low to keep warm. Meanwhile, prepare noodles.

3. Empty and drain the packages of the noodles. Rinse with cold water for 20 seconds and drain in a colander.

4. Add noodles to a pot of boiling water and boil for 1 minute. Drain and pat dry with a paper towel.

5. Add the noodles to the warm broth mixture. Add in the ground beef, raising the temperature until everything is warmed through.

6. Garnish with chopped green onions and red pepper flakes.

7. Serve and enjoy.

# Lamb chops with fragrant curry sauce

Preparation time: 15 minutes

Cooking time: 30 minutes

Gross time: 45 minutes

Serves: 4 serves

## Cooking Ingredients:

- 2 racks of lamb, Frenched (2 lbs each)
- 1 teaspoon melted ghee or olive oil
- salt and pepper
- 1– 2 teaspoons garam masala

## Indian Curry Sauce:

- 1 tablespoon ghee (or coconut oil)
- 1 shallot- chopped
- 3 fat garlic cloves- rough chopped
- 1 tablespoon ginger- finely chopped
- ½ teaspoon turmeric
- ½ teaspoon fennel seed
- ½ teaspoon mustard seed
- 1½ cups diced tomatoes (about 2 medium tomatoes)
- 1 can 13 ounce can coconut milk
- 1 teaspoon dry fenugreek leaves – optional, but delicious!
- 1 teaspoon salt
- 1 teaspoon brown sugar or honey
- Garnish- cilantro, toasted fennel seeds, Aleppo chili flakes

## Cooking Instructions:

1. Heat oven to 425F. Remove any excess fat, and pat lamb dry. Brush with melted ghee or olive oil.

2. Sprinkle all sides with salt, pepper and garam masala spice blend (or use Indian curry powder) and place on a baking sheet and set aside.

3. In a medium pot or large fry pan, heat ghee over medium heat. Add shallot, garlic and ginger and stir until golden (3 to 4 minutes).

4. Then add turmeric, fennel seed and mustard seeds and continue cooking for one more minute (stir occasionally).

5. Add diced tomato and their juices. Continue cooking and stirring about 5 more minutes. Add coconut milk, fenugreek leaves, salt, and sugar.

6. Give a good stir, taste, adjust salt. Bring to a simmer, switch heat to low and let simmer while you bake the lamb.

7. Place lamb in the hot oven, roast 10 minutes, flip, cook 10 more minutes, then flip once more and broil for a couple minutes if you like a crispy crust.

8. Remove lamb from oven and set aside for 5-10 minutes, then slice and plate or platter over top the fenugreek sauce.

9. Sprinkle with fresh cilantro, toasted fennel seeds (optional) and chili flakes (Aleppo chili is nice) if you like.

10. Serve immediately and enjoy!

# Grilled lamb chops with charmoula

Preparation time: 10 minutes

Cooking time: 5 minutes

Total time: 15 minutes

Servings: 4 serves

## Cooking Ingredients:

- 8 lamb loin chops
- 1 teaspoon of olive oil
- 2 tablespoons of Ras el Hanout
- salt

## For the Charmoula:

- 2 tablespoons of fresh mint, roughly chopped
- ¼ cup of fresh parsley, roughly chopped
- 2 tablespoons of lemon zest
- 3 cloves garlic, roughly chopped
- ½ teaspoon of smoked paprika (use regular if you don't have smoked)
- 1 teaspoon of red pepper flakes
- ¼ cup of olive oil
- 2 tablespoons of lemon juice
- salt and pepper to taste

## Cooking Instructions:

1. Coat the lamb with olive oil, ras el hanout and salt. (If not using the ras el hanout, season generously with salt, pepper, and a little cumin).

2. Preheat your grill, then grill about 2 minutes per side for medium rare. Set aside. Let the meat rest a few minutes before serving.

3. Gather all of the Charmoula ingredients in a food processor or magic bullet and pulse until a pesto-like consistency. Don't over blend. It shouldn't be completely liquefied.

4. Serve the lamb chops with a generous helping of Charmoula and some fresh lemon zest. Perfect with grilled asparagus and cauliflower puree on the side.

# Greek Lamb Chops with Tzatziki Sauce

Preparation time: 10 minutes

Cooking time: 10 minutes

Total time: 20 minutes

Servings: 4 serves

## Cooking Ingredients:

- 8 lamb chops
- ¼ cup of lemon juice
- 2 tablespoons olive oil
- 1 clove garlic grated
- 1½ teaspoons kosher salt
- ½ teaspoon pepper

## Tzatziki Sauce:

- 2 cups plain Greek yogurt
- 2 cups diced cucumber or shredded
- ½ cup fresh dill minced
- ¼ cup lemon juice
- 2 cloves garlic grated
- ½ teaspoon of salt
- ¼ teaspoon of pepper

## Cooking Instructions:

1. Position the lamb chops on a large platter and pat dry with paper towel.

2. Combine the lemon juice, olive oil, garlic, salt and pepper in a glass dish. Add chops to the bag and seal.

3. Move bag around to make sure lamb chops are well coated with marinade. Marinate meat for 30 minutes or up to overnight.

4. Grill the lamb, let meat sit out at room temperature for 20-30 minutes and pre-heat grill to medium-high heat.

5. Grill 4-5 minutes per side or until meat thermometer reads 155 degrees. Remove from heat and set aside. Let rest 10 minutes before serving.

6. While lamb is resting, combine the ingredient for Tzatziki Sauce in a medium bowl. Check for seasoning and adjust according to your taste.

7. Serve lamb chops with Tzatziki Sauce on the side. Enjoy

# Grilled Lamb Chops with Dijon-Basil Butter

Total time: 20 minutes

## Cooking Ingredients:

- 4 to 6 centre-cut lamb chops – depending on size
- 1 tablespoon of olive oil
- ½ teaspoon of garlic powder
- 1 tablespoon of chopped fresh basil
- 1 clove garlic, minced
- 1 teaspoon of Dijon-style mustard
- 2 tablespoons of soft butter
- Grilled Lamb Chops

## Cooking Instructions:

1. Sprinkle chops with garlic powder, drizzle with oil and allow to sit until ready to cook.

2. Over medium-high, cook on barbecue grill for 2 to 5 minutes per side. When you think they might be close take one off, cut into center and peak.

3. When done to your liking remove from heat, divide basil butter to top each chop and serve.

4. Put garlic and basil into a small bowl, add mustard and butter and mix well. Can be made ahead, shaped into a log, chilled and sliced.

5. Serve and enjoy.

# Lamb Kebabs with Coconut Curry Dipping Sauce

Preparation time: 10 minutes

Cooking time: 15 minutes

Gross time: 25 minutes

## Cooking Ingredients:

- Metric - Cups/Ounces
- Lamb Kebabs
- 800 g ground/minced lamb
- 1 spring onion finely sliced
- 1 teaspoon of dried cumin
- 1 teaspoon of dried coriander/cilantro
- 1 teaspoon of turmeric powder
- Coconut Curry Dipping Sauce
- 250 ml coconut cream
- 2 tablespoons of curry paste/powder to taste
- 12 bamboo or metal skewers

## Cooking Instructions:

1. Combine and mix all the ingredients together with your hands and form into 12 long kebab shapes.

2. Gently push the skewer into the kebab and press firmly. Bake in the oven for 10 to 15 minutes.

3. You can also adopt the method of shallow frying. Mix the curry paste/powder with the coconut cream.

4. Serve on the side or drizzled across the lamb kebabs. Serve with cauliflower rice. Enjoy.

# Kofta

Preparation time: 15 minutes

Cooking time: 15 minutes

Gross time: 30 minutes

Serves: 3 to 4 servings

**Cooking Ingredients:**

- 14 wooden skewers
- 2 tablespoons finely minced garlic
- ¼ cup of red onion shredded on large holes of box grater and squeezed of all liquid
- ¼ cup of fresh parsley minced
- ¼ cup of fresh mint minced
- 1 tablespoon of fresh ginger grated
- ½ teaspoon of kosher salt
- 2 tablespoons of Garam Masala
- 1 pound of ground lamb
- Greek flat bread (sold in bread section of supermarkets) or see our Gluten Free Flat Bread recipe here
- Shredded lettuce
- Diced tomato
- Tzatziki sauce

**Cooking Instructions:**

1. Soak skewers in water for two hours or longer. If using an outdoor grill, heat to medium heat. Or use a ribbed grill pan on your stove.

2. Mix all ingredients except lamb until combined in a medium bowl. Then add lamb and mix just enough to combine without over working the meat.

3. Form into seven oval shaped patties. Place two skewers side by side into each (two makes it easy to flip on grill).

4. Gill over medium heat flipping halfway through to a nicely seared exterior and cooked to your liking on the inside.

5. Place one or two patties on open flat bread and top with shredded lettuce, chopped tomato and a generous drizzle of Tzatziki. Enjoy.

# Ground Pork Tacos

Serves: 1 serving = about 5 wraps

Preparation time: 10 minutes

Cooking time: 15 minutes

Total time: 25 minutes

## Cooking Ingredients:

- 400 grams of ground pork (about 13 ounces.)
- ½ teaspoon of garlic powder
- ½ teaspoon of onion powder
- ½ teaspoon of sea salt
- 1/8 teaspoon of cumin
- 1/8 teaspoon of ground pepper
- 5 tablespoons of salsa
- 5 or more lettuce leaves (I used Boston Red Leaf Lettuce)
- Taco toppings like diced green peppers/red peppers/avocado/onions etc.

## Cooking Instructions:

1. Mix the ground pork and all the seasonings except the salsa in a small bowl. Mix with your hands.

2. Place the meat in a frying pan and turn the heat to medium. Constantly stir the meat making sure to breakup any large pieces.

3. Once the meat is cooked drain the fat from the pan. Then add the salsa and mix.

4. Place the meat on the lettuce wraps and top with your favourite taco toppings.

5. Serve and enjoy.

# Paleo Pork Dumplings

Preparation time: 10 minutes

Cooking time: 15 minutes

Total time: 25 minutes

Serves: 6 serves

## Cooking Ingredients:

- 1 pound of ground Pork
- 3 Green Onions
- ½ head Napa Cabbage
- 4 Garlic cloves
- 1 teaspoon of fresh Ginger
- 2 Bird's Eye Chili Peppers
- 2 tablespoons of Coconut Aminos
- 2 tablespoons of Sesame Oil
- Coconut Oil
- Paleo Thai Dipping Sauce

## Cooking Instructions:

1. Carefully chop the green parts of the green onions and cabbage and mix together.

2. Mince the garlic, ginger, and chili peppers (sans stems) and add them to the scallions and mix well.

3. Pour in the coconut aminos and sesame oil while stirring, then add in the pork and mix thoroughly. Or you can use a food processor and do this all at once.

4. Form about a 1" oval, dumpling shapes with the meat mixture and set aside. Pre-heat 1 tablespoon coconut oil over medium-high (~6) heat.

5. Cook dumplings in a single layer for 2 to 3 minutes on each side, or until the pork is cooked through and no longer pink.

6. Drain on a paper towel and serve hot. Repeat until all of the pork dumplings are cooked.

7. Serve with Paleo Sweet Chili Sauce or Paleo Thai Dipping Sauce for dipping!

# Pork and cashew stir-fry recipe

Preparation time: 5 minutes

Cooking time: 10 minutes

Total time: 15 minutes

Serves: 2 serves

**Cooking Ingredients:**

- ½ pound of (225 g) pork tenderloin, sliced thin
- 1 egg, whisked
- 1 bell pepper, diced
- 1 green onion, diced
- 1/3 cup (40 g) of cashews
- 1 tablespoon (5 g) of fresh ginger, grated
- 3 cloves of garlic, minced
- 1 teaspoon (5 ml) of Chinese chili oil (optional)
- 1 tablespoon (15 ml) of sesame oil (optional)
- 2 tablespoons (30 ml) of gluten-free tamari sauce or coconut aminos
- Salt to taste
- Avocado oil to cook with

**Cooking Instructions:**

1. Add avocado oil into a frying pan and cook the whisked egg. Remove and set it aside on a plate.

2. Add additional avocado oil into the frying pan and cook the pork. Then add in the pepper, onion, and cashews.

3. Sauté until the pork is fully cooked, then add the cooked egg. Then add in the ginger, garlic, chili oil, sesame oil, tamari sauce, and salt to taste.

4. Serve immediately. Enjoy.

# Pork tenderloin

Preparation time: 10 minutes

Cooking Time: 20 minutes

Total time: 30 minutes

Serves: 2 people

## Cooking Ingredients:

- 1 pound of pork tenderloin
- salt and pepper to taste
- 1 tablespoon coconut oil

## Cooking Instructions:

1. First cut the 1-pound pork tenderloin in half. Add coconut oil into a frying pan on a medium heat.

2. After the coconut oil melts, place the 2 pork tenderloin pieces into the pan. Leave the pork to cook on its side.

3. Once that side is cooked, turn using tongs to cook the other sides. Repeat until the pork looks cooked on all sides.

4. Cook all sides of the pork until the meat thermometer shows an internal temperature of just below 145F (63C).

5. Let the pork sit for a few minutes and then slice into 1-inch thick slices with a sharp knife.

6. Serve and enjoy.

# Kalua Pork

Serves:  5 to 6 Serves

Preparation time:  5 minutes

Cooking time:  6 hours

Total time:  6 hours 5 minutes

## Cooking Ingredients:

- 2 pounds of Pork tenderloin
- 10 ounces of Bacon
- ½ teaspoon black lava sea salt

## Cooking Instructions:

1. Set your slow cooker on low for 6 hours. Add bacon on the bottom of the slow cooker and then set the pork tenderloin on top and cover with black see lava salt.

2. Pull the pork with a fork in the slow cooker and mix until well combined.

3. Serve and enjoy.

# Pork egg roll in a bowl

Preparation time: 5 minutes

Cooking time: 25 minutes

Gross time: 30 minutes

Serves: 4 people

**Cooking Ingredients:**

- 2 tablespoons of sesame oil
- 3 cloves of garlic, minced
- ½ cup of onion, diced
- 5 green onions, sliced on a bias (white and green parts)
- 1 pound of ground pork
- ½ teaspoon ground ginger
- sea salt and black pepper, to taste
- 1 tablespoon of Sriracha or garlic chili sauce, more to taste (omit or use a compliant brand for Whole30)
- 14 ounces' bag coleslaw mix
- 3 tablespoons Coconut Aminos or gluten free soy sauce
- 1 tablespoon of rice vinegar
- 2 tablespoons toasted sesame seeds

**Cooking Instructions:**

1. First, heat sesame oil in a large skillet over medium high heat and add the garlic, onion, and white part of the green onions.

2. Sauté until the onions are translucent and the garlic is fragrant. Then add the ground pork, ground ginger, sea salt, black pepper and Sriracha.

3. Cook until the pork is cooked through. Add the coleslaw mix, coconut aminos, and rice wine vinegar.

4. Cook until the coleslaw is soft. Top with green onions and sesame seeds. Serve and enjoy.

# Apple dijon pork chops

Preparation time: 5 minutes

Cooking time: 10 minutes

Gross time: 15 minutes

Serves: 2 people

**Cooking Ingredients:**

- 2 pork chops (320 g)
- 4 tablespoons of ghee (60 ml)
- 2 tablespoons of applesauce (30 ml)
- 2 tablespoons of ghee (30 ml)
- 2 tablespoons of Dijon mustard (30 ml)
- Salt and pepper, to taste

**Cooking Instructions:**

1. Melt the 4 tablespoons of ghee in a large pan. Then add in the pork chops. Position the pork chops on its side so that the fat cooks in the ghee first.

2. Cook for 3-4 minutes on each side. Check the internal temperature of the pork using a meat thermometer. It should be at about 145 F (63 C).

3. When you cut into the pork chops, you'll find it has a medium rare pink inside. If you prefer your pork chops more cooked, then just leave it in there for longer.

4. While waiting, mix the applesauce, melted ghee, and mustard together well.

5. Serve the pork chops with the sauce and season with salt and pepper to taste.

# Bacon Covered Meatloaf

Preparation time: 15 minutes

Cooking time: 50 minutes

Total time: 1 hour 5 minutes

## Cooking Ingredients:

- Metric - Cups/Ounces
- 1 spring onion sliced
- 2 cloves garlic crushed
- 750 g mince/ground beef
- 750 g mince/ground pork
- 2 eggs - medium lightly beaten
- handful fresh parsley chopped
- handful fresh basil chopped
- 2 slices bacon diced
- 2 tablespoons of sun-dried tomatoes chopped
- 2 teaspoons of dried oregano
- salt and pepper to taste
- vegetables of choice diced/grated/shredded
- 6 slices bacon to cover the meatloaf
- Optional - if not paleo you can add 100g / 3.5 grated cheese of choice to the meatloaf mixture

## Cooking Instructions:

1. Start with oiling and lining a baking tray. Then mix all the ingredients in a large mixing bowl. Mix with your hand thoroughly.

2. Form a large meatloaf shape on the lined baking tray and cover with the bacon slices and sprinkle on parmesan cheese (optional).

3. Bake at 180C/350F for 50 minutes or until thoroughly cooked in the centre.

4. Serve and enjoy.

# Italian parmesan breaded pork cutlets

Preparation time: 5 minutes

Cooking time: 15 minutes

Total time: 20 minutes

Serves: 6 people

## Cooking Ingredients:

- 6 pork cutlets
- ½ cup of Italian dressing
- ½ cup of grated parmesan
- 1 tablespoon of pork seasoning
- 1 to 2 tablespoons of Golden Ghee

## Cooking Instructions:

1. Preheat a medium-sized frying pan to medium heat. Melt your ghee (or butter).

2. Then set up two bowls, one for your Italian dressing, and one for your seasoning and grated parmesan.

3. Coat each cutlet by dipping it in the Italian dressing and then your seasoning/parmesan. Do in a bowl. Set aside on some plates.

4. Depending on the size of your pan, you may need to cook them in batches because it's important not to crowd the pan.

5. Then add 1 tablespoon of ghee or butter and let melt. Add your cutlets to the pan and cook for about 3 to 5 minutes on each side

6. Do this for all until they're all done, and garnish with more parmesan and fresh herbs (optional).

7. Serve and enjoy.

# Pork Chops & Cabbage

Preparation time: 5 minutes

Cooking time: 15 minutes

Total time 20 minutes

Servings: 2 serves

## Cooking Ingredients:

- The Pork Chops
- 2 boneless pork chops
- 1/8 teaspoon of coriander ground
- 1/8 teaspoon of garlic powder
- 1/8 teaspoon of sea salt
- 1 teaspoon of ghee
- The Cabbage
- 6 ounces of cabbage sliced into strips
- 1 tablespoon of apple cider vinegar
- ¼ cup of chicken broth
- 1/8 teaspoon of red chili flakes
- sea salt to taste

## Cooking Instructions:

1. Season pork chops with coriander, garlic powder, and sea salt. Season each side.

2. Melt ghee in a cast-iron skillet over medium heat and cook pork chops for 4 to 5 minutes on each side. Set aside to rest 5 minutes prior to slicing.

3. Add cabbage, vinegar, broth, and sea salt in a medium skillet and boil over high heat.

4. Cook until the liquid has cooked off and the edges of the cabbage begin to brown (stir occasionally).

5. Serve pork chops sliced with cabbage on the side. Enjoy.

# Cajun pork sauté recipe with peppers and tomatoes

Preparation time: 5 minutes

Cooking time: 20 minutes

Total time: 25 minutes

Serves: 2 serves

## Cooking Ingredients:

- 1-pound of Cajun shredded pork, cooked
- 2 bell peppers, sliced
- 1 onion, sliced (optional)
- 1 14 ounces (400g) can of diced tomatoes (or use 2 to 3 fresh tomatoes)
- 4 cloves garlic, minced
- salt to taste
- coconut oil to cook with

## Cooking Instructions:

1. Cook the bell peppers and onions in 1 tablespoon of coconut oil.

2. Add the shredded pork followed by the tomatoes. Simmer for 5 more minutes, then add in the minced garlic and season with salt to taste.

3. Cook for 2 more minutes and serve. Enjoy.

# Dry Rub Pork Spare Ribs

Serves:  4 servings

Preparation time:  15 minutes

Cooking time:  3 hours 30 minutes

Total time:   3 hours 45 minutes

## Cooking Ingredients:

- 2 tablespoons of Cacao
- 1 tablespoon of coriander
- ½ teaspoon of cumin
- ½ teaspoon of cinnamon
- ½ teaspoon of chili powder
- ½ teaspoon of black pepper
- ½ to 1 tablespoon of sea salt
- 2 racks ribs

## Cooking Instructions:

1. Preheat your oven to 350 degrees. Add all the ingredients into a bowl and mix with a spoon thoroughly.

2. Lightly apply this rub to both sides of your rack until it is well coated. Next take two sheets of aluminium foil and sandwich the ribs.

3. Place them in your oven to bake for 3 to 3.25 hours. The meat should be falling off the bone by the time they are done.

4. Serve and enjoy.

# Meatballs

Serves: 4 people

Preparation time: 20 minutes

Cooking time: 30 minutes

Total time: 50 minutes

**Cooking Ingredients:**

**For the meatballs:**

- 1 pound of ground beef
- 1 clove garlic, minced
- ½ cup of shredded mozzarella
- ¼ cup freshly grated Parmesan, plus more for serving
- 2 tablespoons of freshly chopped parsley
- 1 large egg, beaten
- 1 tsp. kosher salt
- ½ tsp. freshly ground black pepper
- 2 tbsp. extra-virgin olive oil

**For the sauce:**

- 1 medium onion, chopped
- 2 cloves garlic, minced
- 1 (28 ounces) can crushed tomatoes
- 1 tsp. dried oregano
- Kosher salt
- Freshly ground black pepper

**Cooking Instructions:**

1. Combine the beef, garlic, mozzarella, Parmesan, parsley, egg, salt and pepper in a large bowl and form 16 meatballs.

2. Heat oil in a large skillet over medium heat. Add meatballs and cook. Turn occasionally, until golden on all sides, about 10 minutes.

3. Remove from skillet and set aside on a paper towel-lined plate. To the same skillet, add onion and cook until soft, 5 minutes.

4. Add garlic and cook until fragrant, 1 minute more. Add tomatoes and oregano and season with salt and pepper.

5. Then add meatballs back to skillet, cover and simmer until sauce has thickened, 15 minutes.

6. Garnish with Parmesan before serving. Enjoy.

# Meatloaf

Servings: 6 servings

Preparation time: 15 minutes

Gross time: 1 hour 15 minutes

## Cooking Ingredients:

- Cooking spray
- 1 tablespoon of extra-virgin olive oil
- 1 medium onion, chopped
- 1 stalk celery, chopped
- 3 cloves garlic, minced
- 1 teaspoon of dried oregano
- 1 teaspoon of chili powder
- 2 pound of ground beef
- 1 cup shredded cheddar
- ½ cup of almond flour
- ¼ cup of grated Parmesan
- 2 eggs
- 1 tablespoon of low-sodium soy sauce
- Kosher salt
- Freshly ground black pepper
- 6 thin strips bacon

## Cooking Instructions:

1. Start by heating the oven to 400°. Grease a medium baking dish with cooking spray.

2. In a medium skillet over medium heat, heat oil. Then add onion and celery and cook until tender. Cook for 5 minutes.

3. Add in garlic, oregano, and chili powder and cook until fragrant, 1 minute (stir gently). Let mixture cool slightly.

4. Combine your ground beef, vegetable mixture, cheese, almond flour, Parmesan, eggs, soy sauce in a large bowl and season with salt and pepper.

5. Shape into a large loaf in baking dish, then lay bacon slices on top and cook until bacon is crispy and beef is cooked through, about 1 hour.

6. Cover dish with foil if the bacon is cooking too quickly.

7. Serve and enjoy.

# Burger Fat Bombs

Preparation time: 15 minutes

Cooking time: 15 minutes

Gross time: 30 minutes

**Cooking Ingredients:**

- Cooking spray, for muffin tin
- 1 pound of ground beef
- ½ teaspoon of garlic powder
- Kosher salt
- Freshly ground black pepper
- 2 tablespoons of cold butter, cut into 20 pieces
- ¼ (8 ounces) block cheddar cheese, cut into 20 pieces
- Lettuce leaves, for serving
- Thinly sliced tomatoes, for serving
- Mustard, for serving

**Cooking Instructions:**

1. Heat oven to 375°. Grease a mini muffin tin with cooking spray. Season beef with garlic powder, salt, and pepper in a medium bowl.

2. Insert about 1 tablespoon of beef into the bottom of each muffin tin cup, completely covering the bottom.

3. Place a piece of butter on top then press about 1 tablespoon of beef over butter to completely cover.

4. Add a piece of cheese on top of meat in each cup then press remaining beef over cheese to completely cover.

5. Allow it to bake until meat is cooked through, about 15 minutes. Let cool slightly.

6. Release each burger from the tin with a metal offset spatula. Do it gently.

7. Serve with lettuce leaves, tomatoes, and mustard. Enjoy.

# Taco Stuffed Avocados

Serves: 4 to 6 People

Preparation time: 10 minutes

Cooking time: 15 minutes

Gross time: 25 minutes

**Cooking Ingredients:**

- 4 ripe avocados
- Juice of 1 lime
- 1 tablespoon of extra-virgin olive oil
- 1 medium onion, chopped
- 1 pound of ground beef
- 1 packet taco seasoning
- Kosher salt
- Freshly ground black pepper
- 2/3 cup shredded Mexican cheese
- ½ cup shredded lettuce
- ½ cup quartered grape tomatoes
- Sour cream, for topping

**Cooking Instructions:**

1. Halve and pit avocados. Use spoon to create a large well by scooping out a bit of the avocado.

2. Dice removed avocado and set aside to use later. Squeeze lime juice over all avocados (to prevent browning!).

3. Heat oil in a medium skillet over medium heat. Add onion and cook until it softens, about 5 minutes.

4. Then add ground beef and taco seasoning, breaking up the meat with a wooden spoon.

5. Season with salt and pepper, and cook until the beef is no longer pink, about 6 minutes. Remove from heat and drain fat.

6. Fill each avocado half with beef, then top with reserved avocado, cheese, lettuce, tomato, and a dollop sour cream.

7. Serve and enjoy.

# Taco Casserole

Serves: 6 People

Preparation time: 15 minutes

Cooking time: 45 minutes

Total time: 1 hour

## Cooking Ingredients:

- 1 tablespoon of extra-virgin olive oil
- ½ yellow onion, diced
- 2 pounds ground beef
- 2 tablespoons of kosher salt
- Freshly ground black pepper
- 2 tablespoons of keto taco seasoning mix
- 1 jalapeño, seeded and minced, plus more sliced for garnish
- 6 large eggs, lightly beaten
- 2 cups of shredded Mexican cheese
- 2 tablespoons of freshly chopped parsley leaves
- 1 cup of sour cream, for serving (optional)

## Cooking Instructions:

1. Preheat oven to 350°. Heat oil in a large skillet over medium heat. Add onion and cook until tender (2 minutes).

2. Add ground beef and season with salt and pepper. Then cook, and break up meat with a wooden spoon, until it is no longer pink (6 minutes).

3. Sprinkle in taco seasoning and jalapeño and cook, stirring, until spices are lightly toasted (1 minute). Drain and let cool slightly.

4. Whisk eggs in a large mixing bowl, then add in meat mixture and spread mixture into an even layer in the bottom of a 2-quart baking dish.

5. Sprinkle with cheese and bake until set, about 25 minutes. Then sprinkle parsley and top each slice with a dollop of sour cream and jalapeno.

6. Serve and enjoy.

# Ice burgers

Serves: 4 people

Cooking time: 20 minutes

Preparation time: 10 minutes

Total time: 30 minutes

## Cooking Ingredients:

- 1 large head iceberg lettuce
- 4 slices bacon
- 1 red onion, sliced
- 1 pound of ground beef
- Kosher salt
- Freshly ground black pepper
- 4 slices cheddar
- 1 tomato, sliced
- Ranch dressing, for serving

## Cooking Instructions:

1. Start with slicing 8 large rounds from the edges of the head of iceberg to create buns.

2. Cook bacon in a large skillet over medium heat until it is crispy. Remove and place on a paper towel-lined plate to drain, reserving bacon fat in pan.

3. Add onion slices and cook until it softens (about 3 minutes per side). Set aside red onions and wipe skillet clean.

4. Return skillet over medium-high heat and shape ground beef into 4 large burger patties.

5. Season both sides of patties with salt and pepper and add to skillet. Cook until seared on both sides and cooked to your liking (4 minutes per side for medium).

6. Top each burger with a slice of cheese, then cover skillet with a lid and cook until cheese has melted, about 1 minute more.

7. Top one iceberg round with the cooked cheeseburger, a slice of bacon, and a tomato slice, then sprinkle with ranch. Top with second iceberg round.

8. Repeat with remaining ingredients and serve. Enjoy.

# Andouille Sausage & Rice Stuffed Pork Tenderloin

Preparation time: 20 minutes

Cooking time: 30 minutes

Gross time: 50 minutes

Serves: 3 to 4 people

**Cooking Ingredients:**

- 4 tablespoons butter, ghee or coconut oil, divided
- 2 garlic cloves, minced
- 1 yellow onion, minced
- 1 red bell pepper, finely chopped
- 2 chicken Andouille sausages, chopped
- 1 small cauliflower, riced*
- 1 cup of chicken broth
- 1 teaspoon of fine sea salt
- ½ teaspoon of smoked paprika
- ½ teaspoon of chili powder
- ½ teaspoon of red pepper flakes
- 1 6 ounces can of tomato paste
- 1 to 1½ pound pork tenderloin

**Cooking Instructions:**

1. First, heat oven to 375 degrees.

2. Over medium heat, place 2 tablespoons of butter in a large fry pan. Add minced garlic and onion and sauté until onions are translucent.

3. Then add red pepper and sausage to the pan and cook for 3 to 4 minutes then add rice cauliflower and 1 cup of broth.

4. Then add all spices and salt. Mix and cook for about 10 minutes, until cauliflower cooks and becomes tender.

5. Lastly, add tomato paste and cook for a couple minutes until it is warm. Cut pork tenderloin open lengthwise.

6. Use about 1 cup of rice mixture and spread out lengthwise down the middle of the tenderloin.

7. Wrap tenderloin around the rice then tie multiple ties around the tenderloin to keep it secure.

8. Add 2 more tablespoons of butter to another large sauté pan over medium-high. Once hot, sear pork tenderloin on all side for about 2 minutes per side.

9. Place on a baking sheet, uncovered for 30 minutes, until meat thermometer reads 160 degrees.

10. Remove and let stand for 10 minutes before removing string and slicing it.

11. Serve with reheated Andouille rice. Enjoy.

# CHAPTER 3: FISH AND SEAFOODS RECIPES

## Fish Curry with Coconut and Spinach

Preparation time: 5 minutes

Cooking time: 20 minutes

Gross time; 25 minutes

Servings: 5 to 6 serves

### Cooking Ingredients:

- Metric - Cups/Ounces
- 1 kg firm white fish cut into cubes
- 2 to 4 tablespoons of curry paste of choice
- 400 ml coconut cream
- 400 ml water
- 500 g spinach washed and sliced

### Cooking Instructions:

1. Heat the oil in a large saucepan, add the curry paste and sauté on a moderate heat for 2 to 3 minutes to activate the spices.

2. Add the coconut cream and water, and bring to the boil. Then carefully add the fish pieces and reduce the heat. Cook for 10 to 15 minutes.

3. Add the prepared spinach and cook for another 3 to 4 minutes.

4. Serve in large bowls. Enjoy.

# Buttered Cod

Preparation time: 5 minutes

Cooking time: 5 minutes

Gross time: 10 minutes

Servings: 4 serves

**Cooking Ingredients:**

**Cod;**

- 1½ pounds of cod fillets
- 6 tablespoons of unsalted butter, sliced

**Seasoning;**

- ¼ teaspoon of garlic powder
- ½ teaspoon of table salt
- ¼ teaspoon of ground pepper
- ¾ teaspoon of ground paprika
- Few lemon slices
- Herbs, parsley or cilantro

**Cooking Instructions:**

1. Make Buttered Cod in Skillet; Stir together ingredients for seasoning in a small bowl.

2. Cut cod into smaller pieces, if desired. Season all sides of the cod with the seasoning.

3. At medium-high heat, heat 2 tablespoons of butter in a large skillet. Once butter melts, add cod to skillet. Cook for 2 minutes.

4. Set heat down to medium. Turn cod over, top with remaining butter and cook another 3 to 4 minutes.

5. Butter will completely melt and the fish will cook. (Don't overcook the cod, it will become mushy and completely fall apart.)

6. Drizzle cod with fresh lemon juice. Top with fresh herbs, if desired.

7. Serve immediately. Enjoy, friends.

# Garlic Shrimp Asparagus Skillet

Serves: 4 people

Preparation time: 10 Minutes

Cooking time: 15 Minutes

Gross time: 25 Minutes

**Cooking Ingredients:**

- 1 pound of uncooked extra-large shrimp — peeled, 454g
- Kosher salt and freshly ground black pepper to taste
- A pinch of crushed red pepper or red pepper flakes
- 1 teaspoon of onion powder
- 2 tablespoons of grass-fed ghee butter or extra virgin olive oil
- 1 tablespoon of extra virgin olive oil
- 3 cloves garlic — minced
- 2 cups of mushrooms — sliced
- 1 bunch of asparagus — ends trimmed and cut in half
- 1 tablespoon fresh parsley — chopped

**Cooking Instructions:**

1. Mix the shrimp, salt, pepper, red pepper flakes, and onion powder in mixing bowl. Mix everything well.

2. In a cast iron skillet, add 2 tablespoons of olive oil or grass-fed ghee butter over medium heat.

3. Add the garlic, and sauté for 30 seconds. Then add the shrimp, and sauté for about 4 minutes or until the shrimp are cooked through and done. Set aside.

4. In the same skillet, add 1 tablespoon of olive oil and the mushrooms. Sauté for 5 minutes. Then, add the asparagus, and cook until it's soft. Stir occasionally.

5. Add the shrimp back to the skillet, and mix everything well to combine.

6. Garnish with fresh parsley. Enjoy!

# Grilled Salmon with Creamy Pesto Sauce

Servings: 4 Serves

Preparation time: 15 minutes

Cooking time: 10 minutes

Total time: 25 minutes

**Cooking Ingredients:**

- 4 to 6 (6 ounces) skin on or skinless salmon fillets
- Olive oil, for brushing salmon and grill
- Salt and freshly ground black pepper
- 4 ounces of cream cheese, diced into small cubes
- ¼ cup of milk
- 3 tablespoons of homemade or store-bought pesto, plus more for serving* (I used homemade)

**Cooking Instructions:**

1. Preheat a grill over medium-high heat to about 425 degrees.

2. Rub both sides of salmon with olive oil (about 1 tablespoon total) and season both sides with salt and pepper.

3. Brush grill grates with oil and grill salmon. Do this for about 3 minutes per side or to desired doneness (if using skin-on salmon grill skin side up first).

4. While waiting for the salmon is, heat cream cheese with milk in a saucepan set over medium heat, stirring constantly until melted.

5. Remove from heat and stir in pesto. Serve salmon warm with creamy pesto sauce.

6. Spoon about 1 teaspoon of pesto over creamy pesto sauce for added flavour.

# Lobster Bisque

Preparation time: 10 minutes

Cooking time: 40 minutes

Gross time: 50 minutes

Servings: 6 people

**Cooking Ingredients:**

- 4 lobster tails frozen in shells (or fresh)
- 2 tablespoons of olive oil extra virgin
- ½ cup of onion chopped
- 1½ teaspoons of garlic minced
- 1 cup of dry white wine
- 2 teaspoons of Worcestershire sauce
- 1 teaspoon of celery salt
- 1 teaspoon of dried thyme
- ½ teaspoon of paprika
- ½ teaspoon of ground cayenne pepper
- ¼ teaspoon of ground black pepper
- 1 tablespoon of tomato paste increase to 2 tablespoons for more tomato flavour
- 2 cups of lobster stock
- 2 cups of heavy cream
- 4 tablespoons of butter

**Cooking Instructions:**

1. Boil lobster tails until shells are bright red. Remove tails to cool and reserve water to use as lobster stock.

2. Remove meat from shells then return the shell to water and boil for another 10 minutes. Using fine mesh strainer, strain lobster stock and reserve 2 cups.

3. Chop lobster meat into bite sized pieces. Set aside. Heat a sauce pan over medium high heat and add olive oil. Sauté onion and garlic, cook for 5 minutes.

4. Slowly add the wine, then stir in the Worcestershire, celery salt, thyme, paprika, cayenne pepper, and black pepper. Stir gently.

5. Stir in the tomato paste and reserved lobster stock. Cook for 10 minutes. Puree mixture in blender or use a stick blender in the pot until smooth.

6. Pour mixture back to the pot, if needed, and add in the heavy cream and butter. Add additional salt if needed.

7. Add lobster meat and continue to simmer for another 5 to 10 minutes. Serve and enjoy.

# Lobster roll salad

Serves: 4 people

**Cooking Ingredients:**

**For the lobster salad:**

- 2 cups of cooked lobster meat, chopped into bite sized pieces
- 1½ cups of cauliflower florets, cooked until tender and chilled
- ½ cup of sugar free mayonnaise
- 1 teaspoon of fresh tarragon leaves, chopped

**To serve:**

- 8 fresh romaine lettuce leaves
- ½ cup of chopped tomatoes
- ½ cup of cooked bacon, chopped

**Cooking Instructions:**

1. Gather and mix the cooked lobster, cooked cauliflower, mayonnaise and tarragon in a medium bowl. Stir until well mixed and creamy.

2. Lay the lettuce leaves on a platter. Divide the lobster salad mixture between the 8 leaves. Sprinkle with chopped tomatoes and chopped bacon.

3. Serve cold or at room temperature. Enjoy.

# Lemon garlic steamed clams

Preparation time: 25 minutes

Cooking time: 5 minutes

Total time: 30 minutes

Serves: Serves 2

## Cooking Ingredients:

- 2 pounds of fresh clams
- 1 cup chicken stock
- 3 cloves garlic, minced
- 1 small onion, diced
- 2 tablespoons of grass-fed butter or ghee
- 2 tablespoons of chopped fresh flat-leaf parsley
- ½ lemon, juiced
- ½ teaspoon of dried thyme (I use this brand)
- ½ teaspoon of sea salt
- ½ teaspoon of crushed red pepper flakes

## Cooking Instructions:

1. Before cooking, add salt to a bowl of water and soak the clams for 20 minutes. The salt will help draw the sand out of the clams.

2. Mix the clams, chicken stock, garlic, onions, butter, a tablespoon of the parsley, lemon juice, thyme, sea salt, and red pepper flakes in a large pot.

3. Boil over medium-high heat, cover and cook until the clams have opened. About 3 to 5 minutes.

4. Pour clams and broth into large bowl and garnish with the remaining parsley and any extra lemon.

5. Serve and enjoy friends.

# Spicy Mussels in Tomato Chorizo Broth

Servings: 6 serves

Preparation time: 5 minutes

Cooking time: 20 minutes

Total time: 25 minutes

**Cooking Ingredients:**

- 1 pound of chorizo or other spicy sausage casings removed
- 3 garlic cloves minced
- ¼ teaspoon of red pepper flakes
- 1 14- oz. can diced tomatoes
- 1 cup Apothic White Winemaker's Blend
- ¼ teaspoon of dried thyme
- 2 pounds of mussels cleaned (discard any that have cracked shells or are open and won't close when tapped gently on counter)
- Salt and pepper to taste

**Cooking Instructions:**

1. Set a large pot or Dutch oven over medium heat, brown sausage until cooked through, and break up any chunks with the back of a wooden spoon.

2. Remove sausage to a paper towel-lined plate to drain (use a slotted spoon), leaving drippings in pan.

3. Add garlic and red pepper flakes to pot and cook until fragrant, about 1 minute.

4. Add tomatoes, wine, and dried thyme and turn heat to medium high. Bring to a boil and add mussels.

5. Cover and cook for 3 minutes. Remove lid, stir gently and re-cover. Cook another 3 to 4 minutes, or until most mussels have opened.

6. Remove mussels from pot with a slotted spoon or skimmer. Return sausage to pot.

7. Season broth with salt and pepper and bring back to a boil for a few minutes until it thickens.

8. Place mussels in large bowls and spooning sauce over. Enjoy.

# Garlic Lemon Butter Crab Legs Recipe

Preparation time: 10 minutes

Cooking time: 5 minutes

Gross time: 15 minutes

Servings 2 people

## Cooking Ingredients:

- 1 pound of king crab legs
- ½ stick salted butter, melted (4 tablespoons)
- 3 cloves garlic, minced
- 1 tablespoon of chopped parsley
- ½ tablespoon of lemon juice
- lemon slices

## Cooking Instructions:

1. Preheat oven to 375F.

2. Thaw the crab legs if they are frozen. Cut or slice the crab legs into halves to expose the flesh. Arrange them evenly on a baking sheet or tray.

3. Melt the butter in a microwave, for about 30 seconds. Add the garlic, parsley and lemon juice to the melted butter. Give a good stir.

4. Drizzle and spread the butter mixture on the crab. Save some for dipping. Bake the crab legs in the oven for about 5 minutes.

5. Serve immediately with the remaining garlic lemon butter and lemon slices. Squeeze some lemon juice on the crab before eating. Enjoy friends.

# Crab Rangoon Fat Bombs

Preparation time: 5 minutes

Cooking time: 15 minutes

Gross time: 20 minutes

## Cooking Ingredients:

- 1 Pkg. 80 ounces Cream Cheese
- 1 can crab 170 g
- ¾ cup of Shredded Mozzarella Cheese
- ½ teaspoon of Finely Minced Garlic
- ½ teaspoon of Garlic Powder
- ½ teaspoon of Onion Powder
- Dash of Salt and Pepper
- 10 Slices Bacon

## Cooking Instructions:

1. Soften the Cream Cheese.

2. Then in a large bowl combine it with the strained canned crab, the shredded mozzarella cheese, the garlic and onion powder and the salt and pepper.

3. Mix until well combined. Place the bowl in the fridge for ½ hour. Cook the bacon until it is Crispy. Then set aside to cool. Then chop into small pieces.

4. Scoop 1 tablespoon size balls of the cream cheese and crab mixture, then use your fingers to make them ball shaped.

5. Roll the balls in the chopped-up bacon. (I washed my hands between each ball.) Store in the fridge until ready to serve.

6. Makes 24 Bacon Crab Rangoon Fat Bombs.

7. Serve and enjoy.

# Ginger Sesame Glazed Salmon

Cooking time: 25 minutes

Preparation time: 15 minutes

Total time: 40 minutes

## Cooking Ingredients:

- 10 oz. Salmon Filet
- 2 tablespoons of Soy Sauce (or coconut aminos)
- 2 teaspoons of Sesame Oil
- 1 tablespoon of Rice Vinegar
- 1 teaspoon of Minced Ginger
- 2 teaspoons of Minced Garlic
- 1 tablespoon of Red Boat Fish Sauce
- 1 tablespoon of Sugar Free Ketchup
- 2 tablespoons of White Wine

## Cooking Instruction:

1. Combine all of the ingredients except for sesame oil, ketchup and white wine in a small Tupperware container.

2. Marinade ingredients in the liquids for about 10 to 15 minutes. Then add sesame oil to a high heated pan.

3. Add fish skin when you see the first wisp of smoke. Let fish cook and skin crisp, then flip and cook on the other side (about 3-4 minutes per side).

4. Add all marinate liquids to the pan and let it boil with the fish when you flip it. Bring out the fish from the pan and set aside.

5. Add ketchup, and white wine to marinate liquids. Cook for 5 minutes to reduce. Serve on the side. Enjoy.

# Creamy Dill Sauce with Salmon or Trout

Preparation time: 10 minutes

Cooking time: 5 minutes

Total time: 15 minutes

Serves: 4 People

## Cooking Ingredients:

### Dill Sauce:

- ¾ cup of sour cream (1)
- 2 teaspoons of Dijon or hot English mustard (2)
- ½ teaspoon of garlic powder or 1 small garlic clove, minced
- 2½ tablespoons of fresh dill, finely chopped
- 1 teaspoon of lemon zest
- 1 to 2 tablespoon of lemon juice
- 2 tablespoons of milk (or olive oil, for richness)
- ¼ to ½ teaspoon of salt
- ½ teaspoon of white sugar

### Fish:

- ½ to 1 tablespoon of oil
- 4 salmon or trout fillets (125g / 4 ounces each)
- Salt and pepper

## Cooking Instructions:

1. Gather all the Dill Sauce ingredients together and mix well to loosen the sour cream. Set aside for 10 minutes. If using fresh garlic, set aside for 20 minutes.

2. Pat fish dry with paper towel. Sprinkle with salt and pepper. Over medium high heat, add oil to skillet and place the fish skin side down.

3. Cook for 2 minutes, then flip and cook the other side for 1½ or 2 minutes. Remove from skillet onto serving plates.

4. Serve with Dill Sauce on the side, garnished with fresh dill and lemon wedges if desired. Enjoy.

# Stew with Oyster Mushrooms

Servings: 4 serves

Preparation time: 20 minutes

Cooking time: 8 hours

Total time: 8 hours 20 minutes

**Cooking Ingredients:**

- 2 tablespoons of lard or coconut oil
- 1 medium onion, chopped
- 1 clove garlic, chopped
- 2 pounds of pork loin, cut into 1" cubes and patted dry
- ½ teaspoon of Himalayan salt
- ½ teaspoon of freshly cracked black pepper
- 2 tablespoons of dried oregano
- 2 tablespoons of dried mustard
- ½ teaspoon of freshly ground whole nutmeg
- 1½ cups bone broth
- 2 tablespoons of white wine vinegar
- 2 pounds of oyster mushrooms
- ¼ cup full fat coconut milk
- ¼ cup ghee
- 3 tablespoons capers

**Cooking Instructions:**

1. Over high heat, melt the lard or coconut oil in a heavy skillet.

2. Add the meat in a single layer, making sure that the pieces do not touch, and cook until brown on all sides.

3. Repeat in several batches if you have to so you don't overcrowd the pan. Remove the cooked pieces of meat to a bowl to collect the juices and set aside.

4. Turn the heat to medium, add a little fat to the pan if necessary, then throw in the onion and garlic and cook until the onion is fragrant.

5. Add oregano, mustard, ground nutmeg, stir to coat then add broth and white wine vinegar.

6. Then add meat and juices back into the pan, bring to a simmer then transfer to slow cooker and cook for 6 hours on low or high for 4 hours.

7. Add an extra cup of water and add mushrooms and continue cooking for 1 hour on high or 2 hours on low.

8. Ladle a little bit of the cooking liquid into a measuring cup. Whisk in coconut milk and ghee then return to slow cooker.

9. Lastly, add capers, mix one final time and serve. Enjoy.

# Salmon with avocado and basil

Preparation time: 7 minutes

Cooking time: 8 minutes

Gross time: 15 minutes

Serves: 4 serves

**Cooking Ingredients:**

- 2 teaspoons of coconut oil
- 1½ teaspoons of coarse kosher salt, divided
- 1 teaspoon of Italian seasonings
- ½ teaspoon of crushed red pepper
- ¼ teaspoon of ground black pepper
- 1½ pounds of boneless salmon filet, skin removed
- 1 avocado
- ¼ cup of chopped basil
- 1 tablespoon lime juice
- chopped scallions, for garnish

**Cooking Instructions:**

1. Over medium high heat, heat oil in a large cast-iron skillet.

2. Sprinkle ¾ teaspoon salt, Italian seasonings, crushed red pepper and black pepper all over the salmon.

3. Place the salmon filet skinned side up in the hot oil. Let cook, undisturbed until browned and crispy along the bottom edge.

4. Turn the salmon over and remove skillet from heat. Allow salmon to remain in hot skillet to allow the carry-over heat to continue cooking.

5. While waiting, peel pit and mash avocado with basil, lime juice and the remaining ¾ teaspoon salt.

6. Serve salmon topped with avocado mash sprinkled with scallions if desired.

# Maple Walnut Crusted Salmon

Serves: Serves 4

Cooking time: 3 hours

Preparation time: 20 minutes

Total time: 3 hours 20 minutes

## Cooking Ingredients:

- 2 tablespoons of ghee (or make your own) for pan
- 4- 175g salmon fillets
- Sprinkle of salt and pepper
- Maple Walnut Crust
- ½ cup of finely chopped walnuts
- 1 teaspoon of smoked paprika
- ½ teaspoon of chipotle powder
- ½ teaspoon of onion powder
- ½ teaspoon of cracked black pepper
- 3 tablespoons of pure maple syrup
- 1 tablespoons of apple cider vinegar
- 1 teaspoon of coconut aminos

## Cooking Instructions:

1. Mix all the ingredients listed under "Maple Walnut Crust" in a small mixing bowl and stir until well combined.

2. Lay your salmon fillets on a plate and spoon the mixture over each piece of fish. Place in the refrigerator, uncovered, for 2 to 3 hours.

3. Preheat your oven to 425F. Melt the ghee in a large oven-safe skillet and set over high heat.

4. Add the pieces of fish and let them cook undisturbed for about 2 minutes, to sear the skin nice and good.

5. Transfer the pan to the oven and continue cooking the fish for about 5 to 8 minutes, depending on desired doneness and thickness of the fillets.

6. Drizzle with a little bit of melted ghee and additional maple syrup at the moment of serving, if desired. Enjoy.

# Sweet Chilli Salmon

Serves: Serves 4

Preparation time: 5 minutes

Cooking time: 5 minutes

Total time: 10 minutes

## Cooking Ingredients:

- 4 x fillets of salmon (approximately 125-150 grams each)
- Oil for searing
- For the marinade
- ¼ cup of liquid aminos (can use soy sauce)
- small handful of baby spinach, chopped very finely
- 1 tsp. black pepper
- 2 tsp. red pepper flakes (optional)
- For the sweet chilli sauce topping
- ¼ cup of homemade chili sauce
- 2 tsp. sesame oil
- 1 tsp. liquid aminos (can use soy sauce)

## Cooking Instructions:

1. In a small bowl, make the marinade and mix well. In a separate bowl, make the sweet chilli sauce topping. Set aside.

2. Coat a large frying pan with oil and heat on medium. Once hot and nice, quickly coat the salmon fillets in the marinade before adding to the pan.

3. Sear on each side for 1 to 3 minutes. Remove from the pan and cover in aluminium foil for 3 minutes to rest.

4. Evenly divide the sweet chilli sauce topping amongst the four salmon fillets.

5. Serve and enjoy.

# Buttered Cod in Skillet

Preparation time: 5 minutes

Cooking time: 5 minutes

Gross time: 10 minutes

Serves: 4 servings

**Ingredients:**

**Cod:**

- 1½ pounds of cod fillets
- 6 tablespoons of unsalted butter, sliced

**Seasoning:**

- ¼ teaspoon of garlic powder
- ½ teaspoon of table salt
- ¼ teaspoon of ground pepper
- ¾ teaspoon of ground paprika
- Few lemon slices
- Herbs, parsley or cilantro

**Cooking Instructions:**

1. Make Buttered Cod in Skillet; Stir together the ingredients for seasoning in a small bowl.

2. Then cut cod into smaller pieces, if desired. Season all sides of the cod with the seasoning.

3. Over medium-high heat, heat 2 tablespoons of butter in a large skillet. Once butter melts, add cod to skillet and cook for 2 minutes.

4. Set heat down to medium. Turn cod over, top with remaining butter and cook another 3 to 4minutes.

5. Butter will completely melt and the fish will cook. (Don't overcook the cod, it will become mushy and completely fall apart.)

6. Drizzle cod with fresh lemon juice. Top with fresh herbs, if desired.

7. Serve immediately. Enjoy, friends.

# Baked Butter Garlic Shrimp

Preparation time: 10 minutes

Cooking time: 20 minutes

Total time: 30 minutes

Serves: 5 to 6 people

## Cooking Ingredients:

- 1 pound of raw shrimp, peeled and cleaned
- 5 tablespoons softened butter
- 3 to 4 large cloves garlic, crushed
- salt and fresh ground pepper
- fresh or dried parsley for garnish
- Lemon wedges, for serving, if desired

## Cooking Instructions:

1. First heat oven to 425 degrees. Smear butter evenly over the bottom of the baking dish.

2. Add the crushed garlic over the butter, sprinkle evenly. Add the shrimp, trying not to overlap if possible

3. Sprinkle everything with salt and pepper. Bake for 7 minutes and then stir the shrimp and bake for 7 to 10 more minutes, or until shrimp is done.

4. Garnish with parsley, if desired, and squeeze a lemon wedge over it, if desired.

5. Serve as a side with steak, or toss the cooked shrimp and butter sauce with pasta. Enjoy.

# Baked Lobster Tails with Garlic Butter

Preparation time: 10 minutes

Cooking time: 15 minutes

Total time: 15 minutes

Serves: 4 serves

## Cooking Ingredients:

- 4 lobster tails
- 5 cloves garlic, minced
- ¼ cup grated Parmesan, plus more for serving
- Juice of 1 lemon
- 1 teaspoon of Italian seasoning
- 4 tablespoons of melted butter

## Cooking Instructions:

1. Preheat oven to 350 degrees F. Mix together garlic, Parmesan, Italian seasoning, and melted butter and season with salt in a bowl.

2. Using sharp scissors or knife, cut the clear skin off the lobster and rub the lobster tails with the garlic butter seasoning.

3. Line a baking sheet with parchment and place the lobster tails. Bake the lobster tails for 15 minutes.

4. The lobster meat inside will be firm and opaque. Internal temperature should read 140 to 145 degrees.

5. Serve immediately friend. Enjoy.

# Cucumber Dill Salmon

Cooking time: 20 minutes

Preparation time: 10 minutes

Total time: 30 minutes

## Cooking Ingredients:

- Olive oil
- 3 to 4 salmon filets
- Salt and pepper
- 1 lemon cut in 6 wedges
- 1/3 cup English cucumber cut in pea size cubes
- 4 ounces of light or Greek yogurt cream cheese
- 2 tablespoons of fresh dill minced
- ¼ cup + an additional 2 to 3 tablespoons of skim milk

## Cooking Instructions:

1. Pre-heat the oven to 400 degrees.

2. Drizzle olive oil into pan and warm over medium heat. Pat moisture from salmon using a paper towel and season with salt and pepper.

3. Sear the salmon on both sides then squeeze the juice from one lemon wedge over the top of the salmon pieces.

4. Bake the salmon 6 to 8 minutes. Remove the salmon from the pan onto a serving platter and on top of the stove over low-medium heat.

5. Add the milk and cream cheese to the same skillet then season with salt and pepper.

6. Combine ¼ cup of the skim milk and cream cheese using an 'S' motion (if the mixture is too thick, add more milk one tablespoon at a time).

7. Switch off the heat and add the diced cucumber and 1 tablespoon of the fresh dill (stir well). Spoon the creamy dill sauce over the salmon filets.

8. Garnish with the additional dill and serve with a lemon wedge. Enjoy.

# CHAPTER 4: DESSERT RECIPES

## Keto Avocado Pops

Preparation time: 0 hours 5 minutes

Cooking time: 6 hours 5 minutes

Total time: 6 hours 10 minutes

**Cooking Ingredients:**

- 3 ripe avocados
- Juice of 2 limes (about 1/3 cup)
- 3 tablespoons of Swerve or other sugar alternative
- ¾ cup coconut milk
- 1 tablespoon of coconut oil
- 1 cup of keto friendly chocolate (such as Lily's)

**Cooking Instructions:**

1. Combine avocados with lime juice, Swerve, and coconut milk into a blender or food processor. Blend until it is smooth.

2. Pour into Popsicle mould. Freeze until firm, 6 hours up to overnight. Combine chocolate chips and coconut oil in a medium bowl.

3. Microwave until melted, then let cool to room temperature. Dunk frozen pops in chocolate and serve. Enjoy.

# Chocolate Covered Strawberry Cubes

Preparation time: 5 minutes

Cooking time: 4 hours 10 minutes

Total time: 4 hours 15 minutes

**Cooking Ingredients:**

- 2 c. chocolate chips
- 2 tbsp. coconut oil
- 16 fresh strawberries with stems (depending on your ice cube tray)

**Cooking Instructions:**

1. Combine and stir together melted chocolate chips and coconut oil in a medium bowl.

2. Spoon a layer of chocolate mixture into the bottom of each ice cube mould, then top each with a strawberry, stem side-up.

3. Spoon remaining chocolate mixture over strawberries.

4. Freeze until chocolate is solid, 4 to 5 hours. Serve and enjoy.

# Chocolate Blueberry Clusters

Preparation time: 15 minutes

Cooking time: 10 minutes

Total time: 25 minutes

## Cooking Ingredients:

- 1½ cup of semisweet chocolate chips, melted
- 1 tablespoon of coconut oil
- 2 cups of blueberries
- Flaky sea salt, for garnish

## Cooking Instructions:

1. Line a small baking sheet with parchment paper. Mix melted chocolate with coconut oil in a medium bowl.

2. Spoon a small dollop of chocolate on the parchment and top with 4 to 5 blueberries.

3. Drizzle chocolate over blueberries and sprinkle with sea salt.

4. Freeze until set, 10 minutes. Serve and enjoy.

# Carrot Cake Keto Balls

Preparation time: 5 minutes

Cooking time: 10 minutes

Total time: 15 minutes

## Cooking Ingredients:

- 1 (8 ounces) block cream cheese, softened
- ¾ cup coconut flour
- 1 teaspoon of stevia
- ½ teaspoon of pure vanilla extract
- 1 teaspoon of cinnamon
- ¼ teaspoon of ground nutmeg
- 1 cup of grated carrots
- ½ cup of chopped pecans
- 1 cup of shredded unsweetened coconut

## Cooking Instructions:

1. Using a hand mixer, beat together cream cheese, coconut flour, stevia, vanilla, cinnamon, and nutmeg in a large bowl. Fold in carrots and pecans.

2. Fold into 16 balls then roll in shredded coconut and serve.

# Keto Chocolate Truffles

Preparation time: 10 minutes

Cooking time: 20 minutes

Gross time: 30 minutes

**Cooking Ingredients:**

- 1 cup of dark chocolate chips, melted
- 1 medium avocado, mashed
- 1 teaspoon of vanilla extract
- ¼ teaspoon of Kosher salt
- ¼ cup of cocoa powder

**Cooking Instructions:**

1. Combine melted chocolate with avocado, vanilla, and salt in a medium bowl. Stir together until smooth and fully combined.

2. Place in the refrigerator to make it firm up slightly (15 to 20 minutes).

3. When chocolate mixture has stiffened, use a small cookie scoop or small spoon to scoop approximately 1 tablespoon chocolate mixture.

4. Roll chocolate in the palm of your hand until round, then roll in cocoa powder. Serve and enjoy.

# Peanut Butter Cheesecakes Bites

Preparation time: 10 minutes

Additional time: 20 minutes

Total time: 30 minutes

## Cooking Ingredients:

- 8 ounces of cream cheese, softened
- ¼ cup of powdered erythritol
- 1 teaspoon of vanilla extract
- ¼ cup of heavy whipping cream
- ¼ cup of peanut butter
- ¾ cup of Lily's Sugar Free chocolate (I used 1.5 bars)
- 2 teaspoons of coconut oil

## Cooking Instructions:

1. Mix cream cheese, erythritol, and heavy whipping cream until smooth. Mix in peanut butter and vanilla extract until fully combined, set aside.

2. Melt chocolate and mix with coconut oil. Brush silicone cups with chocolate mixture and place in freezer for 5 minutes.

3. Repeat previous step and freeze for 10 minutes. Then place a couple spoonful of cheesecake fluff into cup and freeze for 15 minutes.

4. Top cups with chocolate to cover cheesecake fluff. Freeze for another 20 minutes covered or refrigerate for 1 hour.

5. Serve and enjoy.

# Coconut Crack Bars

Preparation time: 2 minutes

Cooking time: 3 minutes

Gross time: 5 minutes

## Cooking Ingredients:

- 3 c. Shredded unsweetened coconut flakes
- 1 c. coconut oil, melted
- ¼ c. monk fruit sweetened maple syrup can substitute for any liquid sweetener of choice

## Cooking Instructions:

1. Line an 8 x 8-inch pan or 8 x 10-inch pan with parchment paper and set aside. Alternatively, you can use a loaf pan.

2. Add your shredded unsweetened coconut in a large mixing bowl. Add your melted coconut oil and monk fruit sweetened maple syrup.

3. Mix until a thick batter remains. If it is too crumbly, add a little extra syrup. Pour the coconut crack bar mixture into the lined pan.

4. Then lightly wet your hands and press firmly into place. Refrigerate or freeze until it is firm. Cut into bars and enjoy!

# Chocolate Chip Cookies

Preparation time: 15 minutes

Cooking time: 15 minutes

Gross time: 30 minutes

**Cooking Ingredients:**

- 2 large eggs
- ½ cup (1 stick) of melted butter
- 2 tablespoons of heavy cream
- 2 teaspoons of pure vanilla extract
- 2¾ cups of almond flour
- ¼ teaspoon of kosher salt
- ¼ cup of keto-friendly granulated sugar (such as Swerve)
- ¾ cup of dark chocolate chips (such as Lily's)
- Cooking spray

**Cooking Instructions:**

1. First heat the oven to 350°. Whisk the egg with the butter, heavy cream, and vanilla in a large bowl. Stir in the almond flour, salt, and Swerve.

2. Fold the chocolate chips into the cookie batter. Line baking sheet with parchment, form the batter into 1" balls and arrange 3" apart on baking sheets.

3. Grease the bottom of a glass with cooking spray and flatten the balls with the bottom of the glass.

4. Bake until the cookies are golden, about 17 to 19 minutes.

5. Serve and enjoy.

# Sugar-Free Cheesecake

Preparation time: 15 minutes

Cooking time: 7 hours 45 minutes

Gross time: 8 hours 0 minutes

## Cooking Ingredients:

- ½ cup of almond flour
- ½ cup of coconut flour
- ¼ cup of shredded coconut
- ½ cup (1 stick) of butter, melted
- 3 (8 ounces) blocks cream cheese, softened to room temperature
- 16 ounces of sour cream, at room temperature
- 1 tablespoon of stevia
- 2 teaspoons of pure vanilla extract
- 3 large eggs, at room temperature
- Sliced strawberries, for serving

## Cooking Instructions:

1. First heat oven to 300°. Make the crust by greasing an 8" or 9" spring form pan, and cover the bottom and edges with foil.

2. Mix together the flours, coconut, and butter in a medium bowl. Press the crust into the bottom and a little up the sides of the prepared pan.

3. Place the pan in the fridge. Then make the filling by mixing the cream cheese and sour cream together, then beat in the stevia and vanilla.

4. Add the eggs one at a time, mixing after each addition. Spread the filling evenly over the crust.

5. Place cheesecake in a deep roasting pan and set on middle rack of oven. Carefully pour enough boiling water into roasting pan to come halfway up sides of spring form pan.

6. Bake for 1 hour to 1 hour 20 minutes. Switch oven off, but leave the cake in the oven with the door slightly ajar to cool slowly for an hour.

7. Remove pan from water bath and take off foil, then let chill in the fridge for at least five hours or overnight. Slice and garnish with strawberries. Enjoy.

# Keto Ice Cream

Preparation time: 5 minutes

Cooking time: 8 hours

Gross time: 8 hours 15 minutes

**Cooking Ingredients:**

- 2 (15 oz.) cans coconut milk
- 2 cups of heavy cream
- ¼ cup of swerve confectioner's sweetener
- 1 teaspoon of pure vanilla extract
- Pinch kosher salt

**Cooking Instructions:**

1. Place the coconut milk in the fridge at least 3 hours (preferably overnight).

2. Spoon coconut cream into a large bowl, leaving liquid in can, and use a hand mixer to beat until creamy. Then set aside.

3. Beat heavy cream until soft peaks form in a large bowl using a hand mixer. Beat in sweetener and vanilla.

4. Fold whipped coconut into whipped cream, then transfer mixture into a loaf pan.

5. Freeze until solid, about 5 hours. Enjoy.

# Chocolate Mug Cake

Serves: 1 Serve

Preparation time: 5 minutes

Cooking time: 5 minutes

Total time: 10 minutes

**Cooking Ingredients:**

- 2 tablespoons of butter
- ¼ cup of almond flour
- 2 tablespoons of cocoa powder
- 1 large egg, beaten
- 2 tablespoons of keto friendly chocolate chips, such as Lily's
- 1 teaspoon of swerve sweetener
- ½ teaspoon of baking powder
- Pinch kosher salt
- ¼ cup of whipped cream, for serving

**Cooking Instructions:**

1. Heat the butter in a microwave-safe mug. Heat until melted (30 seconds).

2. Add remaining ingredients except whipped cream and stir until it is well combined.

3. Cook for 45 seconds to 1 minute, or until cake is set but still fudgy.

4. Top with whipped cream before serving. Enjoy.

# Peanut Butter Cookies

Preparation time: 5 minutes

Cooking time: 5 minutes

Total time: 10 minutes

## Cooking Ingredients:

- 1½ cup of smooth unsweetened peanut butter, melted (plus more for drizzling)
- 1 cup of coconut flour
- ¼ cup of coconut sugar
- 1 teaspoon of pure vanilla extract
- Pinch kosher salt
- 2 cups of dark chocolate chips, melted
- 1 tablespoon of coconut oil

## Cooking Instructions:

1. Combine peanut butter, coconut flour, coconut sugar, vanilla and salt in a medium bowl. Stir well until smooth.

2. Using a small cookie scoop, form mixture into rounds then press down lightly to flatten and place on baking sheet lined with parchment paper.

3. Freeze until firm, about 1 hour. Whisk together melted chocolate and coconut oil in a medium bowl.

4. Dip peanut butter rounds in chocolate until fully coated then return to baking sheet (use a fork).

5. Drizzle with more peanut butter then freeze for about 10 minutes.

6. Serve cold. Store any leftovers in the freezer. Enjoy.

# Keto Frosty

Serves: 4 Servings

Preparation time: 10 minutes

Cooking time: 35 minutes

Total time: 45 minutes

## Cooking Ingredients:

- 1½ cups of heavy whipping cream
- 2 tablespoons of unsweetened cocoa powder
- 3 tablespoons of keto-friendly powdered sugar sweetener, such as Swerve
- 1 teaspoon of pure vanilla extract
- Pinch kosher salt

## Cooking Instructions:

1. Combine cream, cocoa, sweetener, vanilla, and salt in a large bowl.

2. Using a hand mixer, beat mixture until stiff peaks form. Scoop mixture into a Ziploc bag and freeze 30 to 35 minutes.

3. Cut tip off a corner of the Ziploc bag and pipe into serving dishes. Enjoy.

# Chocolate Mousse

Serves: Serves 2

Preparation time: 15 minutes

Cooking time: 1 hour

Gross time: 1 hour 15 minutes

**Cooking Ingredients:**

- 2 ripe avocados
- ¾ cup of heavy cream
- ½ cup of keto-approved chocolate chips (we love Lily's)
- ¼ cup of honey or your favourite keto sweetener
- 3 tablespoons of unsweetened cocoa powder
- 1 teaspoon of vanilla
- ½ teaspoon of kosher salt

**Cooking Instructions:**

1. Blend all ingredients except chocolate curls until smooth in a food processor or blender.

2. Transfer to serving glasses and refrigerate 30 minutes and up to 1 hour.

# Avocado Brownies

Preparation time: 5 minutes

Cooking time: 25 minutes

Gross time: 30 minutes

## Cooking Ingredients:

- 4 large eggs
- 2 ripe avocados
- ½ cup (1 stick) of butter, melted
- 6 tablespoons of unsweetened peanut butter
- 2 teaspoons of baking soda
- 2/3 cup of coconut sugar (or 18 packets Stevia)
- 2/3 cup of unsweetened cocoa powder
- 2 teaspoons of pure vanilla extract
- ½ teaspoon of kosher salt
- Flaky sea salt (optional)

## Cooking Instructions:

1. First heat oven to 350° and line an 8"-x-8" square pan with parchment paper.

2. Combine all ingredients except flaky sea salt in a blender or food processor and blend until smooth.

3. Transfer batter to prepared baking pan and smooth top with a spatula. Top with flaky sea salt, if using.

4. Bake until brownies are soft (20 to 25 minutes) but not at all wet to the touch.

5. Let cool 25 to 30 minutes before slicing and serving. Enjoy.

# Chocolate Keto Protein Shake

Serves: Serves 1

Preparation time: 5 minutes

Cooking time: 5 minutes

Total time: 10 minutes

**Cooking Ingredients:**

- ¾ cup of almond milk
- ½ cup of ice
- 2 tablespoons of almond butter
- 2 tablespoons of unsweetened cocoa powder
- 2 to 3 tablespoons of keto-friendly sugar substitute to taste (such as Swerve)
- 1 tablespoon of chia seeds, plus more for serving
- 2 tablespoons of hemp seeds, plus more for serving
- ½ tablespoon of pure vanilla extract
- Pinch kosher salt

**Cooking Instructions:**

1. Combine all ingredients in blender or a food processor and blend until smooth.

2. Pour into a glass and garnish with more chia and hemp seeds.

3. Serve and enjoy.

# Double Chocolate Muffins

Serves: 1 dozen

Preparation time: 10 minutes

Cooking time: 15 minutes

Total time: 25 minutes

## Cooking Ingredients:

- 2 cups of almond flour
- ¾ cup of unsweetened cocoa powder
- ¼ cups of swerve sweetener
- 1½ teaspoon baking powder
- 1 teaspoon of kosher salt
- 1 cup (2 sticks) of butter, melted
- 3 large eggs
- 1 teaspoon of pure vanilla extract
- 1 cup of sugar-free dark chocolate chips, such as Lily's

## Cooking Instructions:

1. First heat oven to 350° and line a muffin tin with liners. In a large bowl whisk together almond flour, cocoa powder, Swerve, baking powder, and salt.

2. Add melted butter, eggs, and vanilla and stir until combined. Fold in chocolate chips.

3. Divide batter between muffin liners and bake until a toothpick inserted into the middle comes out clean, 12 minutes.

4. Serve and enjoy.

# Cookie Dough Keto Fat Bombs

Preparation time: 5 minutes

Cooking time: 1 hour

Total time: 1 hour 5 minutes

**Cooking Ingredients:**

- 8 tablespoons (1 stick) of butter, softened
- 1/3 cup of Keto friendly confectioners' sugar (such as Swerve)
- ½ tsp. vanilla extract
- ½ tsp. kosher salt
- 2 cups of almond flour
- 2/3 cups of Keto friendly dark chocolate chips (such as Lily's)

**Cooking Instructions:**

1. Beat butter until light and fluffy in a large bowl using a hand mixer. Add sugar, vanilla and salt and beat until well combined.

2. Gently beat in almond flour until no dry spots remain, then fold in chocolate chips.

3. Cover the bowl with plastic wrap and place in refrigerator to firm slightly (15 to 20 minutes).

4. Using a small cookie scoop, scoop dough into small balls. Store in the refrigerator or in the freezer. Enjoy.

## Sugar-Free Nutella

Preparation time: 10 minutes

Cooking time: 10 minutes

Total time: 20 minutes

Servings: Serves 6

**Cooking Ingredients:**

- ¾ cup of hazelnuts toasted and husked**
- 2 to 3 tablespoons of melted coconut oil can sub avocado oil
- 2 tablespoons of cocoa powder
- 2 tablespoons of powdered Swerve Sweetener
- ½ teaspoon of vanilla extract
- Pinch salt

**Cooking Instructions:**

1. Grind hazelnuts in a food processor or high-powered blender until finely smooth and beginning to clump together.

2. Add 2 tablespoons of oil and continue to blend until nuts smoothen out into a butter. Add remaining ingredients and blend until well combined.

3. If the mixture is very thick, add an additional tablespoon oil.

4. Serve and enjoy.

# CHAPTER 5: SOUP & STEWS RECIPES

## Bacon Cheeseburger Soup

Cooking time: 40 minutes

Preparation time: 20 minutes

Total time: 60 minutes

**Cooking Ingredients:**

- 5 slices Bacon
- 12 ounces of Ground Beef (80/20)
- 2 tablespoons of Butter
- 3 cups of Beef Broth
- ½ teaspoon of Garlic Powder
- ½ teaspoon of Onion Powder
- 2 teaspoons of Brown Mustard
- 1½ teaspoon of Kosher Salt
- ½ teaspoon of Black Pepper
- ½ teaspoon of Red Pepper Flakes
- 1 teaspoon of Cumin
- 1 teaspoon of Chili Powder
- 2½ tablespoons of Tomato Paste
- 1 medium Dill Pickle, diced
- 1 cup of Shredded Cheddar Cheese
- 3 ounces of Cream Cheese
- ½ cup of Heavy Cream

**Cooking Instructions:**

1. Start with cooking the bacon in a pan until crispy, then set aside.

2. Add ground beef in the bacon fat and cook until browned on one side, flip and cook other side until brown.

3. Place beef in a pot, and move it to the sides. Add butter and spices to the pan and let the spices sweat for 30 to 45 seconds.

4. Then add beef broth, tomato paste, mustard, cheese, and pickles to the pot and let cook for a few minutes until it melts.

5. Cover pot and turn to low heat. Cook for another 20 to 30 minutes. Turn stove off, then finish with heavy cream and crumbled bacon. Stir well and serve. Enjoy.

**Nutrition:** Calories, 48.6g Fats, 3.4g Net Carbs, and 23.4g Protein.

# Roasted Garlic Soup

Preparation time: 10 minutes

Cooking time: 55 minutes

Total time: 65 minutes

Serves: 6 Servings

## Cooking Ingredients:

- 2 bulbs of garlic
- 1 tablespoon extra-virgin olive oil, divided
- 3 shallots, chopped
- 1 large head of cauliflower, chopped (approximately 5 cups)
- 6 cups of gluten-free vegetable broth
- ¾ teaspoon of sea salt
- Freshly ground pepper, to taste

## Cooking Instructions:

1. First heat oven to 400F. Peel the outer layers of the garlic bulb. Cut off about ¼-inch from the top of the bulb.

2. Place in on a square of aluminium foil and coat each with ½ teaspoon of olive oil. Heat in the oven for 35 minutes.

3. Once complete, allow to cool slightly before removing from aluminium foil and squeezing out the garlic from each clove.

4. Meanwhile, pour remaining olive oil in a medium-sized saucepan. Turn heat to medium-high and add chopped shallots. Fry until tender for about 6 minutes.

5. In the saucepan, add the roasted garlic along with remaining ingredients. Cover and bring to a boil.

6. Bring down the heat to low and cook for 15 to 20 minutes until the cauliflower is tender.

7. Drop mixture into the bowl of your blender. Puree until smooth, about 30 seconds.

8. Adjust with salt and pepper and serve. Enjoy.

# Fat Bomb Hamburger Soup

Preparation time: 30 minutes

Cooking time: 60 minutes

Total time: 1 hour 30 minutes

Serves: 6 servings

**Cooking Ingredients:**

- 125-grams red onion, sliced (approx. ½ onion)
- 125-grams mushrooms, chopped (approx. 10 count)
- 200-grams yellow bell pepper, sliced (approx. 1 count)
- 200 grams Brussels sprouts, halved (approx. 20 count)
- ¼ cup of red palm oil, melted
- Himalayan rock salt, to taste
- Freshly ground pepper, to taste
- 1 pound of grass-fed regular ground beef
- 3 cloves garlic, minced
- 200-grams celery (approx. 6 sticks)
- 4 cups of homemade beef stock, with the fat
- 2 cups of organic whole tomatoes
- 1 tablespoon of organic tomato paste
- 1 bay leaf
- 1 teaspoon of dried oregano
- pinch cayenne pepper or ½ teaspoon chili powder
- 25-grams (¼ cup) fresh parsley, chopped

**Cooking Instruction:**

1. Preheat your oven to 350F. On a large baking sheet, place onions, mushrooms, bell pepper, Brussels sprouts, palm oil, salt and pepper.

2. Place sheet to the oven and roast vegetables for 25 to 30 minutes. Once complete, remove and set aside.

3. In a large soup pot, add ground beef and cook on medium-low heat until just cooked through.

4. Then add garlic and celery, cook for another 3 minutes. Do not drain the fat, keep it in there.

5. Add stock, tomatoes, paste and spices. Bring to a boil, reduce heat to low and simmer for 15 to 20 minutes.

6. Stir in roasted vegetables and chopped parsley. Serve with a slice of Flax Focaccia. Enjoy.

# Mulligatawny

Preparation time: 10 minutes

Cooking time: 30 minutes

Total time: 40 minutes

Serves: 10 servings

**Cooking Ingredients:**

- 10 cups turkey or chicken broth
- 1½ tablespoon of curry powder
- 5 cups of chopped turkey or chicken, cooked
- 3 cups of celery root, riced or chopped finely
- ¼ cup of apple cider or juice
- 2 tablespoons of Swerve sweetener
- ½ cup of sour cream
- ¼ cup of fresh parsley, chopped
- Salt and pepper to taste

**Cooking Instructions:**

1. In a large soup pot, add the broth, curry powder, turkey or chicken, celery root rice, and apple cider.

2. Bring to a boil and simmer for about 25 to 30 minutes. Add the sweetener, sour cream, and fresh parsley and stir well.

3. Taste and season with salt and pepper to taste. Serve hot. Enjoy friend.

**Nutrition**

Information per serving: 214 calories, 4g fat, 4g net carbs, 36g protein.

# Chicken "Noodle" Soup

Preparation time: 10 minutes

Cooking time: 15 minutes

Total time: 25 minutes

Serves: 4 Serves

## Cooking Ingredients:

- 2 tablespoons coconut oil
- 1 pound (453 grams) boneless, skinless chicken thighs
- 1 cup of diced celery* see note
- 1 cup diced carrots
- ¾ cup (approx. 6) chopped green onion, green part only
- 6 cups of chicken stock
- ½ teaspoon of dried basil
- ½ teaspoon of dried oregano
- 1 teaspoon of grey sea salt
- ⅛ teaspoon fresh ground pepper
- 2 cups (300 grams) of spiralized daikon noodles* see note

## Cooking Instructions:

1. To make on a stove top: In a large saucepan, add coconut oil and chicken thighs.

2. Cook on medium for 15 minutes, until chicken is just about cooked through. Then shred with a fork.

3. Add your celery, carrots and onions and cook for another 5 minutes.

4. Add remaining ingredients. Cover and bring to a boil. Reduce heat and simmer for 20 to 25 minutes.

5. Once complete, add daikon noodles and serve. Enjoy.

# Broccoli Cheddar Soup

Cooking Time: 20 minutes

Preparation time: 10 minutes

Total Time: 30 minutes

Serves: 4 Servings; ¾ Cup per Serving

## Cooking Ingredients:

- 2 tbsp. Butter
- 1/ 8 c. White Onion
- ½ teaspoon Garlic, finely minced
- 2 c. Chicken Broth
- Salt and Pepper, to taste
- 1 c. Broccoli, chopped into bite size pieces
- 1 tbsp. Cream Cheese
- ¼ c. Heavy Whipping Cream
- 1 c. Cheddar Cheese; shredded
- 2 Slices Bacon; Cooked and Crumbled (Optional)
- ½ teaspoon xanthan gum (optional, for thickening)

## Cooking Instructions:

1. Sauté onion and garlic with butter in large pot over medium heat until onions are tender and translucent.

2. Add broth and broccoli to pot. Cook broccoli until softened. Add salt, pepper and desired seasoning as necessary.

3. In a small bowl, place cream cheese and heat in microwave for 30 seconds until soft and easily stirred.

4. Stir heavy whipping cream and cream cheese into soup; bring to a boil. Remove from heat and quickly stir in cheddar cheese.

5. Stir in xanthan gum, if desired. Allow to thicken. Serve hot with bacon crumbles. Enjoy.

# French Onion Soup

Preparation time: 10 minutes

Cooking time: 40 minutes

Total time: 50 minutes

Servings: 6 Servings

## Cooking Ingredients:

- 5 tablespoons of Butter
- 500 g Brown Onion Medium
- 2 teaspoons of Natvia (Or Erythritol) 4 drops stevia, or erythritol
- 4 tablespoons of olive oil
- 3 cups of Beef Stock

## Cooking Instructions:

1. Add butter and olive oil in a medium-large pot over medium low heat. Add onions and 1 teaspoon of Salt. Add chopped onions.

2. Cook without lid, stirring often for 20 minutes or until onions are golden brown. Stir in the stevia and cook for another 5 minutes.

3. Add the stock to the saucepan and cook. Turn to a low heat and simmer for 25 minutes.

4. Ladle into soup bowls and serve. Enjoy.

## Nutrition:

Keto French Onion Soup - Keto French Food

Amount per Serving: Calories 212, Calories from Fat; 162% Daily Value*, Total Fat; 18g 14%, Total Carbohydrates; 5g 17%, Protein; 3g 3%.

# Curried Beef Stew

Preparation time: 10 minutes

Cooking time: 30 minutes

Total time: 40 minutes

Serves: 4 servings

**Cooking Ingredients:**

- 1.5 pounds of stew beef meat
- 1 tablespoon of coconut oil
- ½ medium white onion, diced
- 3 teaspoons of minced garlic
- 2 teaspoons of curry powder
- 1 teaspoon of Cumin
- 1 teaspoon of Pink Himalayan Salt
- ½ teaspoon of chili powder
- 1 can coconut milk, refrigerated
- ½ cup of Water
- 4 ounces of cauliflower (optional)

**Cooking Instructions:**

1. Freeze the can of coconut milk until ready to use in the recipe.

2. Heat a large pan over medium-high heat and add ½ tablespoon of coconut oil. Once hot, add in the stew meat pieces and brown on all side.

3. Remove from the pan and set aside in a bowl. Add the ½ tablespoon of coconut oil to hot pan and turn the heat to medium.

4. Scrape up the bottom using a spatula. Add in the diced onion, and cook until translucent. Add in the garlic, curry powder, cumin, salt and chili powder. Mix using the spatula and cook until spices are fragrant.

5. Place the stew meat back in and stir to combine. Remove the coconut milk from the freezer (should have been at least 10 minutes) and open can.

6. Add the hardened coconut milk to the beef mixture and allow it to melt down. Add the water and stir until thoroughly combined.

7. Cover the pan and allow to simmer for 20 minutes. If you are adding in the cauliflower, add it after 10 minutes have passed.

8. Then replace with the lid and allow to cook remaining time. Remove the lid and either serve.  Serve over cauliflower rice. Enjoy!

# Beef Stroganoff Soup

Hands-on: 20 minutes

Cooking time: 40 minutes

Total time: 60 minutes

Serves: 6 servings

**Cooking Ingredients:**

- 2 large beef rump (sirloin) steaks (800 g/ 1.76 lbs.)
- 600 g brown or white mushrooms (1.3 lbs.)
- ¼ cup of ghee or lard (55 g/ 1.9 oz.)
- 2 cloves garlic, minced
- 1 medium white or brown onion, chopped (110 g/ 3.9 oz.)
- 5 cups bone broth or chicken stock or vegetable stock (1.2 l/ quart)
- 2 teaspoons of paprika
- 1 tablespoon of Dijon mustard you can make your own
- Juice from 1 lemon (~ 4 tbsp.)
- 1½ cup sour cream or heavy whipping cream (345 g/ 12.2 oz.) - you can use paleo-friendly coconut cream
- ¼ cup of freshly chopped parsley
- 1 teaspoon of salt
- ¼ teaspoon of freshly ground black pepper
- Optionally, you can use a thickener: 1 tablespoon of ground chia seeds (+ 0.1 g net carbs per serving) or arrowroot powder (+ 1.2 g net carbs per serving) mixed in ¼ cup of water or use cream & egg yolk mixture like I did in my Pork & Kohlrabi Stew.

**Cooking Instructions:**

1. Lay the steaks in the freezer in a single layer for 30 to 45 minutes. This will make it easy to slice the steaks into thin strips.

2. Meanwhile, clean and slice the mushrooms. When the steaks are ready, use a sharp knife and slice them as thin as you can. Season with some salt and pepper.

3. Grease a large heavy bottom pan with half of the ghee and heat. Then, add the beef slices in a single layer. Do not overcrowd the pan.

4. Fry over a medium-high heat until it's cooked through and browned from all sides.

5. Remove the slices from the pan and place in a bowl. Set aside for later. Do the same for the remaining slices.

6. Grease the pan with the remaining ghee. Add in the chopped onion and minced garlic in the pan and cook until lightly browned and fragrant.

7. Add the sliced mushrooms and cook for 3 to 4 more minutes while stirring occasionally.

8. Then add your Dijon mustard, paprika, and pour in the bone broth. Add lemon juice and boil for 2 to 3 minutes. Add the browned beef slices and sour cream.

9. Remove from heat. If you are using a thickener, add it to the pot and stir well. Finally, add freshly chopped parsley.

10. Eat hot with a slice of toasted Keto Bread or let it cool down and store in the fridge for up to 5 days. Enjoy!

**Nutrition:**

Calories from carbs; 7%, protein; 27%, fat; 66%.

Total carbs; 10.8 grams, Fibre 1.4 grams, Sugars 4.8 grams, Saturated fat; 18.4 grams, Sodium; 783 mg (34% RDA), Magnesium; 152 mg (38% RDA), Potassium; 1,398 mg (70% EMR).

# Buffalo Ranch Chicken Soup

Preparation time: 20 minutes

Cooking time: 30 minutes

Total time: 50 minutes

**Cooking Ingredients:**

- 4 cups of Boneless Skinless Chicken Breast
- 2 tablespoons of (I added more to mine, but made it very mild for the family)
- 4 tablespoons of Ranch Dressing
- 2 Celery Stalks (chopped of sliced)
- ¼ cup of Yellow Onion (chopped)
- 6 tablespoons of Butter (salted)
- 8 ounces of Cream Cheese
- 1 cup of Heavy Whipping Cream
- 8 cups of Chicken Broth
- 7 slices of Hearty Bacon

**Cooking Instructions:**

1. First, cook and shred chicken by coating the bottom of a deep-frying pan with olive oil on medium heat. Then place the chicken in pan and cook for 5 minutes.

2. Flip to the other side and add ¾ cup of water. Cover and cook for 7 to 10 minutes (add little drops of water occasionally). Shred after cooling.

3. Cook and crumble bacon. I always precook bacon to make cooking a little easier.

4. While waiting add all ingredients to a saucepan and cook on medium. When chicken and bacon are properly cooked add to the sauce pan and cover.

5. Allow to cook for 5 to 10 minutes before serving. Enjoy.

**Nutrition:**

Calories: 444, Total Fat: 34g, Cholesterol: 133mg, Sodium: 1572mg, Potassium: 3mg, Carbohydrates: 4g, Dietary Fibre = 1g, Net Carbs= 3g, Dietary Fibre 1g, Sugars: 2g (all from natural sources), Protein: 28g

# Chicken Stew

Preparation time: 5 minutes

Cooking time: 2 hours

Gross time: 2 hours 5 minutes

Serves: 4 Servings

**Cooking Ingredients:**

- 2 cups of chicken stock
- 2 medium carrots (½ cup), peeled and finely diced
- 2 celery sticks (1 cup), diced
- ½ onion (½ cup), diced
- 28 ounces skinless and deboned chicken thighs diced into 1" pieces
- 1 spring fresh rosemary or ½ teaspoon dried rosemary
- 3 garlic cloves, minced
- ¼ teaspoon of dried thyme
- ½ teaspoon of dried oregano
- 1 c. fresh spinach
- ½ cup of heavy cream
- salt and pepper, to taste
- xantham gum, to desired thickness starting at ⅛ teaspoon

**Cooking Instructions:**

1. In a 3-quart crockpot, place the chicken stock, carrots, celery, onion, chicken thighs, rosemary, garlic, thyme, and oregano.

2. Cook on low for 4 hours or on high for 2 hours. Add salt and pepper, to taste. Stir in spinach and the heavy cream.

3. Sprinkle and thicken with xantham gum to desired thickness starting at ⅛ teaspoon. Continue to whisk until mix and cook for another 10 minutes.

4. Serve and enjoy.

**Nutrition:**

Calories: 228 Fat: 11 Carbohydrates: 6 Protein: 23

# Chicken Fajita Soup

Servings: 8 serves

Preparation time: 10 minutes

Cooking time: 6 hours 30 minutes

Total time: 6 hours 40 minutes

## Cooking Ingredients:

- 2 pounds of boneless skinless chicken breasts
- 1 cup of chicken broth this is to pour over chicken in slow cooker
- 1 onion chopped
- 1 green pepper chopped
- 3 garlic cloves minced
- 1 tablespoon of butter
- 6 ounces of cream cheese
- 2 10 ounces of cans diced tomatoes with green chilis
- 2½ cups of chicken broth
- ½ cup of heavy whipping cream
- 2½ tablespoons of homemade taco seasoning recipe here or 1 packet of taco seasoning
- salt and pepper to taste

## Cooking Instructions:

1. Add boneless skinless chicken breasts to a slow cooker and cook for 3 hours on high or 6 hours on low in a cup of chicken broth. Season with salt and pepper.

2. When the chicken is done, remove from slow cooker and shred. (You can strain the leftover broth for the soup.)

3. In a large saucepan fry green pepper, onion, and garlic in 1 tablespoon of butter until they are translucent (2 to 3 minutes).

4. Mash the cream cheese into the veggies with a spoon so that it will combine smoothly as it melts.

5. Add the canned tomatoes, chicken broth, heavy whipping cream, and taco seasoning.

6. Cook on low uncovered for 20 minutes. Add chicken, cover and cook for 10 minutes.

7. Add salt and pepper to taste. Serve and enjoy!

## Nutrition:

Calories: 306kcal, Carbohydrates: 8.2g, Protein: 26g, Fat: 17g, Saturated Fat: 9g, Cholesterol: 120mg, Sodium: 880mg, Potassium: 757mg, Fibre: 1.6g, Sugar: 3g, Vitamin A: 12.7%, Vitamin C: 26.5%, Calcium: 4.9%, Iron: 4.4%.

# Italian Wedding Soup

Preparation time: 15 minutes

Cooking time: 25 minutes

Total time: 40 minutes

Servings: 6 serves

**Cooking Ingredients:**

**Meatballs:**

- 1 pound of ground beef OR ground pork
- ½ cup of crushed pork rinds OR almond flour
- ½ cup of grated Parmesan cheese
- 1 teaspoon of Italian seasoning
- ¾ teaspoon of salt
- ½ teaspoon of pepper
- 1 large egg

**Soup:**

- 2 tablespoons of avocado oil
- ¼ cup of chopped onion
- 4 celery stalks chopped
- 1 teaspoon of salt
- ½ teaspoon of pepper
- 3 cloves garlic minced
- 1 teaspoon of dried oregano
- 6 cups of chicken broth
- 2 cups of riced cauliflower
- 2 cups of packed spinach leaves
- Additional salt and pepper
- Parmesan for sprinkling

**Cooking Instructions:**

1. Mix together the ground meat, crushed pork rinds, cheese, Italian seasoning, salt, and pepper in a large mixing bowl.

2. Add the egg and mix well using your hands. Form into ½ inch meatballs and place on a waxed paper-lined tray. Refrigerate until soup is ready.

3. Heat the oil over medium heat until shimmering in a large saucepan or stock pot.

4. Add the onion, celery, salt, and pepper and fry until vegetables are soft and tender (7 minutes). Add the garlic and cook for 1 minute.

5. Stir in the chicken broth and oregano and simmer for 10 minutes. Add the cauliflower rice and the meatballs and cook for about 5 minutes.

6. Add the spinach leaves and cook until wilted, 2 minutes more. Season to taste.

7. Serve and enjoy.

**Nutrition:**

Food energy: 303kcal, Total fat: 20.16g, Calories from fat: 181, Cholesterol: 73mg, Carbohydrate: 5.73g, Total dietary fibre: 1.86g, Protein: 29.48g.

# Cream of Chicken Soup

Preparation time: 10 minutes

Cooking time: 20 minutes

Total time: 30 minutes

Serves: 2 servings

## Cooking Ingredients:

- 2 cups (500 grams) of cauliflower florets
- 2/3 cup (157 mL) of unsweetened original almond milk
- 1 cup (250 mL) of chicken broth
- 1 teaspoon (5 mL) of onion powder
- ½ teaspoon (2.5 mL) of grey sea salt
- ¼ teaspoon (1.23 mL) of garlic powder
- ¼ teaspoon (1.23 mL) of freshly ground black pepper
- 1/8 teaspoon (0.61 mL) of celery seed (optional)
- 1/8 teaspoon (0.61 mL) of dried thyme
- ¼ cup (30 grams) of Beef Gelatin
- ¼ cup (54 grams) of finely diced cooked chicken thighs

## Cooking Instructions:

1. Place all ingredients but cook chicken and gelatin in a small saucepan. Cover and bring to a boil over medium heat.

2. Turn heat to low and cook for about 7 to 8 minutes, until cauliflower is softened. Remove from the heat.

3. Add ½ cup or so of the hot liquid to a medium-sized bowl using a ladle. Add gelatin, one scoop at a time. Stir until dissolved, then add the next scoop.

4. Transfer the cauliflower mixture and gelatin mixture to your food processor, immersion blender or high-powered blender. Blend until totally smooth.

5. Add cauliflower and gelatin mixture back to saucepan. Add cooked chicken to cauliflower and gelatin mixture. Cover and heat on low for 2 to 5 minutes, until it thickens. Serve immediately. Enjoy friend.

## Nutrition:

Calories: 198, Calories from Fat: 62.1, Total Fat: 6.9 g Saturated Fat: 1.1 g, Cholesterol: 24 mg, Sodium: 672 mg, Carbs: 9.4 g, Dietary Fibre: 3.8 g, Net Carbs: 5.6 g, Sugars: 3.3 g, Protein: 26.4 g,

# Coffee and Wine Beef Stew

Serves: 6 servings

Preparation time: 20 minutes

Cooking time: 3 hours 20 minutes

Total time: 3 hours 40 minutes

## Cooking Ingredients:

- Pounds Stew Meat
- 3 c. Coffee
- 1 c. Beef Stock
- 1½ c. Mushrooms (Baby Bella)
- 2/3 c. Red Wine (Merlot)
- 1 Medium Onion
- 3 tbsp. Coconut Oil
- 2 tbsp. Capers
- 2 tsp. Garlic
- 1 tsp. Salt
- 1 tsp. Pepper

## Cooking instructions:

1. Cube all stew meat, then thinly slice onions and mushrooms. Bring 3 tablespoons of coconut oil and heat in a pan on the stove.

2. Season beef with salt and pepper, then brown all of it in small batches. Ensure you don't overcrowd the pan.

3. Once all meat is browned, cook onions, mushrooms, and garlic in the remaining fat in the pan. Do this until onions are translucent.

4. Then mix together coffee, beef stock, red wine, and capers to the vegetables. Stir mixture well.

5. Add beef into the mixture, bring to a boil then reduce heat to low.

6. Cover and cook for 3 hours. Serve and enjoy.

## Nutrition:

504 Calories, 32.2g Fats, 2.7g Net Carbs, and 42.5g Protein.

# Green chicken enchilada soup

Serves: 4 servings

Preparation time: 10 minutes

Cooking time: 5 minutes

Total time: 15 minutes

## Cooking Ingredients:

- ½ cup of salsa Verde (see example)
- 4 ounces of cream cheese, softened
- 1 cup of sharp cheddar cheese, shredded
- 2 cups of bone broth or chicken stock
- 2 cups of cooked chicken, shredded

## Cooking Instructions:

1. Add the salsa, cream cheese, cheddar cheese and chicken stock in a blender and blend until smooth.

2. Pour into a medium saucepan and cook on medium until hot. Add the shredded chicken and cook an additional 3 to 5 minutes until heated through.

3. Garnish with additional shredded cheddar and chopped cilantro if desired. Enjoy.


## NUTRITION:

Serving Size: 1.5 cups, Calories: 346, Fat: 22gCarbohydrates: 3g net, Protein: 32g.

# Beef Stew

Preparation time: 10 minutes

Cooking time: 1 hour

Total time: 1 hour 10 minutes

Serves: 4 servings

## Cooking Ingredients:

- 1 pound of Beef Short Rib
- 2 cups of beef broth
- 4 cloves minced garlic
- 100-gram Onion
- 100-gram carrot
- 100-gram radishes
- ¼ teaspoon of Pink Himalayan Salt
- ¼ teaspoon of pepper
- ½ teaspoon of xanthan Gum
- 1 tablespoon of Butter
- 1 tablespoon of coconut oil

## Cooking Instructions:

1. Cut the short rib into bite sized chunks, salt and pepper and set aside.

2. At medium-high heat, heat a large saucepan and add coconut oil. Then add short rib and brown on all side. Remove from saucepan and set aside.

3. Chop onions, carrots and radishes into bite sized pieces and mince garlic. Add onions, garlic and butter and cook down for a couple minutes.

4. Once the onions are soft, add the broth and combine. Add the xanthan gum and mix.

5. Allow broth mixture to come to boil and then transfer the meat back in and cook covered for 30 minutes. Stir frequently scrapping the bottom as you stir,

6. After 30 minutes add the carrots and radishes and cook for 30 minutes, stirring frequently until it thickens.

7. If you feel the need you can add more broth or some water. Serve warm and enjoy!

## NUTRITION:

Calories: 432.25kcal, Carbohydrates: 5.5g, Protein: 19.25g, Fat: 36.5g, Fibre: 1.5g.

# Green Chile Pork Stew

Preparation time: 15 minutes

Cooking time: 1 hour 30 minutes

Total time: 1 hour 45 minutes

Servings: 8 servings

Calories: 182kcal

## Cooking Ingredients:

- 2 pounds of pork loin (cubed)
- 2 teaspoons ground cumin
- 2 teaspoons granulated garlic
- 1 teaspoon pure ground chili powder optional
- 2 ounces of onion (about ½ cup, chopped)
- 2 cloves garlic
- 1 can whole Hatch green chilies and liquid (27 ounces can)
- 3 tablespoons oil
- 2 cups water
- fried or poached eggs optional

## Cooking Instructions:

1. Heat oil in a big frying pan and brown the cubed pork loin.

2. Chop the onion and garlic. Open the can of chilies and blend with the onion and garlic in a blender until the chilies resemble a thick chunky paste.

3. Add the spices to the browned pork and give a nice stir until fragrant. Pour the pureed chilies, and their juice from the can, over the browned pork.

4. Add the two cups of water, and the liquid from the can. Stir and reduce pan down from medium-low to low heat.

5. Cover the pan with the lid ajar and simmer for 1 to 1 ½. Add water occasionally. It will be very flavourful just by adding water.

6. Adjust seasonings. Ladle into a bowl over cauliflower rice, over zoodles and top with a fried or poached egg (optional). Enjoy.

# CHAPTER 6: SMOOTHIES

## Keto Kale & Coconut Shake

Makes 1 large shake

Preparation time: 5 minutes

Cooking time: 5 minutes

Total time: 10 minutes

**Ingredients:**

- 1 cup unsweetened almond milk (substitute your favourite non-dairy milk)
- ½ cup of full-fat canned coconut milk
- 4 cups chopped kale (you can also do a mix of spinach & kale)
- ¼ cup ground coconut (unsweetened)
- 1 1-inch piece fresh ginger, peeled (optional--skip it if you don't like the taste of ginger)
- ¼ teaspoon kosher salt (or Celtic sea salt if you have it--it's rich in beneficial minerals!)
- 1 cup ice

**Instructions:**

1. Add the almond and coconut milk into base of blender, followed by ginger, kale, ground coconut, salt, and ice.

2. Blend until very smooth. Blend for about 3-5 minutes. Enjoy

# Turmeric Keto Smoothie

Preparation time: 2 minutes

Cooking time: 3 minutes

Total time: 5 minutes

Servings: Serves 1

Calories: 600 kcal

## Ingredients:

- 200 ml full fat coconut milk
- 200 ml unsweetened almond milk
- 1 teaspoon of granulated sweetener (stevia etc) or other sweetener
- 1 tablespoon of ground turmeric
- 1 teaspoon of ground cinnamon
- 1 teaspoon of ground ginger
- 1 tablespoon of MCT Oil or use coconut oil
- 1 tablespoon of Chia seeds to top
- Get Ingredients Powered by Chicory

## Instructions:

1. Throw all the ingredients except the chia seeds in a blender, add some ice and puree until smooth.

2. Sprinkle chia seeds on top and enjoy!

# Avocado Smoothie with Coconut Milk, Ginger, and Turmeric

Preparation time: 10 minutes

Total time: 10 minutes

Servings: Serves 2

Calories: 232kcal

## Ingredients:

- ½ avocado (3-4 ounces)
- ¾ cup full - fat coconut milk (from a can)
- ¼ cup almond milk
- 1 teaspoon of fresh grated ginger (about 1/2-inch piece)
- ½ teaspoon of turmeric
- 1 teaspoon of lemon or lime juice (or more to taste)
- 1 cup crushed ice (or more for a thicker smoothie)
- sugar-free sweetener to taste

## Instructions:

1. Throw in the first 6 ingredients to a blender and blend on low-speed until smooth.

2. Add crushed ice and sweetener. Blend on high until smooth.

3. Taste and adjust sweetness and tartness to your taste, enjoy.

## Nutrition Facts:

Calories 232 Calories from Fat 202% Daily Value*, Total Fat 22.4g 34%, Sodium 25mg 1%, Total Carbohydrates 6.9g 2%, Dietary Fibre 2.8g 11%, Sugars 1.14g, Protein 1.7g 3%

# Vanilla Low Carb Smoothie with Marshmallow

Preparation time: 5 minutes

Cooking time: 5 minutes

Total time: 10 minutes

Serves: 1 to 2 serves

## Ingredients:

- 1 cup water
- 3 cups ice
- ½ cup full-fat coconut milk
- 2 tablespoons collage hydrosolate (I use this one)
- 2 tablespoons ground golden flax (I use this one) or chia
- 1 scraped vanilla bean or 1 teaspoon vanilla extract (gluten free)
- stevia or honey to taste

## Optional ingredients:

- 2 pastured organic eggs
- 3 tablespoons grass fed whey protein (I use this one) OR
- 1 tablespoon colostrum (I use this one)
- 2 tablespoons plantain flour (I use this one)

## Instructions:

1. Throw all the ingredients in a blender and pulse until smooth.

2. Serve and enjoy.

# Chai Pumpkin

Preparation time: 5 minutes

Cooking time: 5 minutes

Total time: 10 minutes

Serves: Serves 1

## Ingredients:

- ¾ cup full-fat coconut milk
- 3 tablespoons pumpkin puree
- 1 tablespoon MCT oil, optional
- 1 teaspoon loose chai tea
- 1 teaspoon alcohol-free vanilla
- ½ teaspoon pumpkin pie spice *see note
- ½ fresh or frozen avocado

## Instructions:

1. Add all ingredients except avocado to the blender and blend well.

2. Add the avocado and blend until broken apart.

3. Serve with a sprinkle of pumpkin spice on top, if you'd like.

## Nutrition Information per Serving:

Calories:726, Calories from Fat:628.2, Total Fat:69.8 g, Saturated Fat:51.2 g, Sodium:54 mg, Carbs:19.5 g, Dietary Fiber:8.2 g, Net Carbs:11.3 g, Sugars:5.6 g, Protein:5.5 g

# Raspberry Avocado Smoothie

Preparation time: 2 minutes

Total time: 2 minutes

Servings: Serves 2

Calories: 227kcal

**Ingredients:**

- 1 ripe avocado peeled and pit removed
- 1 1/3 cup water
- 2 to 3 tablespoons of lemon juice
- 2 tablespoon of low carb sugar substitute I like to use 1/8 teaspoon liquid stevia extract
- ½ cup frozen unsweetened raspberries or other low carb frozen berries

**Instructions:**

1. Add all ingredients to blender and blend until smooth.

2. Pour into two tall glasses and enjoy with a straw!

**Nutrition Facts:**

Amount Per Serving (330 g): Calories 227, Calories from Fat 180% Daily Value, Fat 20g 31%, Sodium 16mg 1%, Total Carbohydrates 12.8g 4%, Dietary Fibre 8.8g 35%, Protein 2.5g 5%.

# Strawberry Lime

Serves: 2 Servings

Preparation time: 5 minutes

Cooking time: 2 minutes

Total time: 7 minutes

**Ingredients:**

- 1 can full fat coconut milk
- 8 ounces frozen strawberries
- ¼ cup egg white protein powder
- 2 tablespoons MCT oil
- 1 tablespoon lime juice, freshly squeezed
- 1 tablespoon sunflower lecithin powder
- ¼ teaspoon stevia

**Instructions:**

1. Place all ingredients in a blender and blend on high speed until smooth.

2. Serve and enjoy.

# Chocolate Coconut Keto Smoothie Bowl

Preparation time: 5 minutes

Cooking time: 5 minutes

Total Time: 10 minutes

Serves: Serves 1

**Ingredients:**

- ¾ cup of full-fat canned organic coconut milk (BPA-free)
- 2 tablespoons unsweetened raw cacao powder or unsweetened cocoa powder
- 15 to 20 drops liquid coconut stevia (or plain stevia to taste)
- Handful of ice (just enough to thicken)
- 2 scoops of collagen protein

**Instructions:**

1. Combine all of the ingredients except the collagen in a blender and blend well.

2. Add the collagen and gently pulse until blended to avoid damaging delicate proteins.

3. Place in a bowl and add optional garnishes. Enjoy.

**Nutrition (Per Serving):**

Calories: 500, Protein: 26g, Total Carbs: 12g, Fibre: 4g, Sugars: 3g, Sugar Alcohols: 0g, Net Carbs: 8g, Fat: 38g, Saturated Fat: 34g, Sodium: 120 mg, Potassium: 244 mg, Calcium: 4%, Iron: 12%.

# Chocolate Mint Avocado Smoothie

Preparation time: 5 minutes

Cooking time: 5 minutes

Total Time: 10 minutes

Serves: Serves 1

## Cooking Ingredients:

- ½ cup of coconut milk
- 1 cup water
- ½ cup of ice
- 2 scoops of Chocolate Collagen Protein
- ½ a frozen avocado
- 4 mint leaves
- 1 tablespoon of crushed cacao butter
- 2 tablespoons of shredded coconut

## Cooking Instructions:

1. Add all ingredients excluding the collagen protein and shredded coconut to a blender. Blend for 45 seconds on high.

2. Add collagen protein and blend for 5 seconds on low. Blend gently to avoid damaging delicate protein.

3. Top with coconut flakes. Enjoy.

## Nutritional Information (per serving):

Calories: 552, Protein: 26g, Carbs: 10g, Fibre: 9g, Sugar:2g, Fat: 44g, Saturated Fat: 25g, Polyunsaturated: 1g, Monounsaturated: 7g, Sodium: 100mg, Potassium: 354mg, Vitamin A: 2mg, Vitamin C: 12mg, Calcium: 3mg, Iron: 4mg.

# Cinnamon chocolate

Preparation time: 5 minutes

Cooking time: 5 minutes

Total time: 10 minutes

Serves: Serves 1

**Ingredients:**

- ¾ cup of coconut milk
- ½ ripe avocado
- 2 teaspoons of unsweetened cacao powder
- 1 teaspoon of cinnamon powder
- ¼ teaspoon of vanilla extract
- Stevia to taste
- ½ teaspoon MCT oil or 1 teaspoon coconut oil (optional)

**Instructions:**

1. Combine and blend all the ingredients together well in a blender.

**Nutrition:**

Calories: 300, Sugar: 2 g, Fat: 30 g, Carbohydrates: 14 g, Fibre: 10 g, Protein: 3 g.

# Chocolate Mint Avocado Smoothie

Preparation time: 5 minutes

Cooking time: 5 minutes

Total time: 10 minutes

Serves: Serves 1

## Ingredients:

- ½ cup coconut milk
- 1 cup water
- ½ cup ice
- 2 scoops of Chocolate Collagen Protein
- ½ a frozen avocado
- 4 mint leaves
- 1 tablespoon of crushed cacao butter
- 2 tablespoons of shredded coconut

## Instructions:

1. Add all ingredients excluding the collagen protein and shredded coconut to a blender. Blend for 45 seconds on high.

2. Add collagen protein and blend for 5 seconds on low. Blend gently to avoid damaging delicate proteins.

3. Top with coconut flakes. Enjoy

## Nutritional Information (per serving):

Calories: 552, Protein: 26g, Carbs: 10g, Fibre: 9g, Sugar:2g, Fat: 44g, Saturated Fat: 25g, Polyunsaturated: 1g, Monounsaturated: 7g, Trans fat: 0g, Cholesterol: 0mg, Sodium: 100mg, Potassium: 354mg, Vitamin A: 2mg, Vitamin C: 12mg, Calcium: 3mg, Iron: 4mg.

# Green Smoothie

Preparation time: 5 minutes

Cooking time: 5 minutes

Total time: 10 minutes

Servings: 2 people

**Ingredients:**

- 1 cup cold water
- 1 cup baby spinach
- ½ cup cilantro
- 1-inch ginger peeled
- ¾ English cucumber peeled
- ½ -1 lemon peeled
- 1 cup frozen avocado

**Instructions:**

1. Add all ingredients to a blender and blend until smooth.

2. Store in an air-tight container in the fridge for up to 3 days. Enjoy.

**Nutrition:** Calories 148, Calories from Fat 99% Daily Value*, Total Fat 11g 17%, Saturated Fat 1g 5%, Sodium 28mg 1%, Potassium 653mg 19%, Total Carbohydrates 13g 4%, Dietary Fibre 6g 24%, Sugars 2g, Protein 2g 4%, Vitamin A 38.1%, Vitamin C 31.8%, Calcium 4.9%, Iron 7.2%.

# Mint Coco Smoothie

Preparation time: 5 minutes

Cooking time: 5 minutes

Total time: 10 minutes

**Ingredients:**

- 4 ounces of full fat coconut milk
- 4 ounces of water
- ½ cup frozen cauliflower
- ½ avocado
- 1 scoop collagen protein
- 1 teaspoon of vanilla extract
- 1 tablespoon of chopped mint
- 1 tablespoon of cacao powder
- 1 tablespoon of coconut oil
- dash of ceylon cinnamon
- dash of himalayan sea salt
- optional toppings coconut flakes, chia seeds, flaxseeds, hemp seeds, pumpkin seeds, sliced macadamia nuts

**Instructions:**

1. Add all ingredients into a blender and blend until very smooth and creamy. Enjoy!

# Cucumber Green Tea Detox Smoothie

Preparation time: 5 minutes

Cooking time: 10 minutes

Total time: 5 minutes

Servings: 2 Serves

## Ingredients:

- 8 ounces of water
- 2 teaspoons of Match Green Tea powder
- 1 cup sliced cucumber
- 2 ounces of ripe avocado
- 1 teaspoon of lemon juice
- ½ teaspoon of lemon liquid stevia
- ½ cup ice
- Get Ingredients Powered by Chicory

## Instructions:

1. Add water and green tea powder into a blender first and give it a whir to combine.

2. Add the remaining ingredients and blend on high until smooth.

3. Taste and adjust sweetener as desired. Enjoy.

## Nutrition Facts:

Amount Per Serving(1 g): Calories 69 Calories from Fat 41% Daily Value*, Total Fat 4.6g 7%, Saturated Fat 0.6g 3%, Sodium 3mg 0%, Total Carbohydrates 6.8g 2%, Dietary Fibre 3.4g 14%, Sugars 1.3g, Protein 2g 4%.

# Lime Pie Smoothie

Preparation time: 5 minutes

Total time: 5 minutes

Servings: 2 Serves

Calories: 340 kcal

## Ingredients:

- 2 cups coconut milk. I used Trader Joe's Coconut Milk, unsweetened. You can add some of my favourite canned milk variety for extra healthy fats too!
- ¼ cup raw cashews soaked if you do not have a high-power blender to pulverize or macadamia nuts, swoon!
- 4 tablespoons lime juice
- ½ avocado
- 2 handfuls spinach or any greens. I also sometimes add a handful of raw cauliflower. Can't taste it, promise!!
- 1 tablespoon erythritol or any favourite low carb sweetener to taste
- 2 tablespoons coconut butter I use my homemade,
- 2 tablespoons chia seeds or hemp hearts, optional
- 2 tablespoons collagen this is the brand I use, use tessa10 for 10% any order
- Splash vanilla extract optional
- Zest of one lime to taste, optional
- Liquid stevia or raw honey to taste I prefer NuNaturals, and use about 10 to 20 drops to taste

## Instructions:

1. Throw all ingredients into a blender and whir until smooth and creamy.

# CHAPTER 7: APPETIZER RECIPES

## Parmesan Zucchini Rounds

Preparation time: 10 minutes

Cooking time: 20 minutes

Total time: 30 minutes

Serves: 12 People

### Cooking Ingredients:

- 3 large zucchinis, sliced (6 cups sliced rounds)
- 1 whole egg
- 1 egg white
- 1½ cups Parmesan cheese, grated
- ¼ cup of fresh parsley, chopped
- ½ teaspoon of garlic powder
- olive oil cooking spray

### Cooking Instructions:

1. Preheat oven to 425 degrees and spray baking sheets with cooking spray.

2. Beat the egg and white in a shallow bowl, set aside. Meanwhile combine the Parmesan, garlic powder and parsley in another bowl and mix well.

3. Dip zucchini rounds in egg mixture then in Parmesan and place on baking sheet. Bake for 10 minutes on both sides.

4. Do not overlap zucchini on the baking sheet. Serve and enjoy.

# Cheddar Cauliflower Bacon Bites

Preparation time: 10 minutes

Cooking time: 15 minutes

Total time: 25 minutes

Servings: 6 Serves

Calories: 172 kcal

## Cooking Ingredients:

- 4 cups cauliflower florets
- 6 ounces of uncured nitrate free bacon cooked till crisp
- 1 egg
- 1 teaspoon baking powder
- ¼ teaspoon salt
- 1/3 cup scallions chopped
- ½ cup coconut flour
- 1 cup shredded cheddar cheese
- Get Ingredients Powered by Chicory

## Cooking Instructions:

1. Start by heating the oven to 400 degrees. Steam cauliflower until tender. Allow to cool then add to food processor.

2. Pulse until fine crumbs, then place in a large bowl and add the rest of the ingredients.

3. Stir until combined. Oil a mini muffin tin. Fill mini muffin cups by adding a heaping tablespoon of batter and pressing into each cup, about 30 cups.

4. Bake for 15 minutes and allow to cool about for 10 minutes then remove from pan.

5. Enjoy immediately!

# Jalapeno Popper Dip

Preparation time: 10 minutes

Cooking time: 30 minutes

Total time: 40 minutes

## Cooking Ingredients:

- 1 pound of bacon, fried, drained, and chopped
- 2 8 ounces of packages reduced fat cream cheese, softened
- ½ cup mayonnaise
- ½ cup Greek yogurt
- 2 tablespoons of sriracha chili sauce
- 4 to 6 jalapenos, deseeded and chopped
- 1½ cups shredded cheese of choice (I used a Mexican blend)
- ½ teaspoon of each onion powder and dill weed

## Topping:

- ¼ cup salted butter, melted
- ½ cup grated parmesan cheese (the kind from the green shake container)
- 6 Light Rye Wasa crackers, crushed (¾ cup crushed pork rinds or Joseph's pita crumbs might work as well)

## Cooking Instructions:

1. Set a small amount of chopped bacon aside for topping. Throw all the dip ingredients in a blender and blend until mostly smooth.

2. Spread the dip into a 10-inch round baking. Combine the topping ingredients and sprinkle evenly on top of the dip. Then top with reserved bacon bits.

3. Bake at 350 degrees F for 20 to 30 minutes.

4. Serve with veggies. Enjoy.

# Cream Cheese Stuffed Meatballs

Preparation time: 15 minutes

Cooking time: 15 minutes

Total time: 30 minutes

**Ingredients**

**Meatballs:**

- 1 spring onion finely sliced
- 1 clove garlic crushed
- 750 g ground/mincemeat. I used pork
- salt and pepper to taste
- 1 egg slightly beaten
- 2 slices bacon finely chopped
- 3 tablespoons of sun-dried tomatoes finely diced
- 2 tablespoon of favourite herbs - I use rosemary, thyme, oregano and sage

**Filling:**

- 110 g cream cheese diced into squares

**Instructions:**

1. In a large mixing bowl combine all the meatball ingredients. Mix thoroughly with your hands.

2. Scoop up a golf ball size of meatball mixture (Use a dessert spoon). Squeeze the mixture into a ball then flatten into a circle.

3. In the centre of the meatball circle, place a cube of cream cheese then fold the meatball mixture around the cream cheese.

4. Place the cream cheese stuffed meatball on a greased baking tray. Do the same for the remaining mixture.

5. Spray them all with olive oil spray so they will crisp and brown beautifully. Place in the oven and bake at 180C/350F for 15 to 20minutes.

6. Serve and enjoy.

# Cucumber Cream Cheese Sandwiches

Preparation time: 5 minutes

Cooking time: 15 minutes

Total time: 20 minutes

Servings:  Serves 20

Calories: 47kcal

## Cooking Ingredients:

- 3 oz. of cream cheese
- 1 medium cucumber
- 1 tbsp. sour cream
- dash salt
- dash pepper
- dash celery salt
- dash garlic powder
- Flaxseed Bread or other low carb bread
- Low Carb Sweeteners | Keto Sweetener Conversion Chart

## Cooking Instructions:

1. Grate cucumber and let drain until most of the liquid is gone. Then mix the cream cheese, medium cucumber, sour cream until smooth.

2. Season with salt, pepper, celery salt and garlic powder. Cut the low carb flax bread squares in half through the middle height of the slice to make them thinner.

3. Spread cucumber mixture on bottom slice and cover with top slice. Cut in half to make finger size.

4. Serve immediately, enjoy.

# Salt and Vinegar Zucchini Chips

Preparation time: 15 minutes

Cooking time: 12 hours

Total time: 12 hours 15 minutes

Servings: Serves 8

## Cooking Ingredients:

- 4 cups thinly sliced zucchini about 2-3 medium
- 2 tablespoons extra virgin olive oil avocado oil or sunflower oil
- 2 tablespoons white balsamic vinegar
- 2 teaspoons coarse sea salt

## Cooking Instructions:

1. Use a mandolin or slice zucchini as thin as possible. Then whisk olive oil and vinegar together in a small bowl.

2. Place zucchini in a large bowl and toss with oil and vinegar. Place zucchini in even layers to dehydrator then sprinkle evenly with coarse sea salt.

3. Depending on how thin you sliced the zucchini and, on your dehydrator, the drying time will vary, about 8 to 14 hours.

4. To make in the oven: Line a cookie sheet with parchment paper. Place zucchini evenly and bake at 200 degrees F for 2 to 3 hours.

5. Rotate half way during cooking time. Store chips in an airtight container. Enjoy.

# Chicken Salad Cucumber Bites

Servings: 8 people

Preparation time: 5 minutes

Cooking time: 20 minutes

Total time: 25 minutes

Calories: 74 kcal

## Cooking Ingredients:

- 1 English cucumber
- 7 oz. cooked chicken breast
- 2 tablespoons of mayonnaise
- 2 scallions chopped
- 2 tablespoons of fresh cilantro
- ¼ teaspoon of ground cumin
- salt and pepper to taste
- Kalamata, black or green olives for topping optional

## Cooking Instructions:

1. Slice the cucumber in squares. Shred your chicken with a food processor if you have one or you can use a fork.

2. In a bowl thoroughly mix the chicken, mayo, cilantro, scallions and cumin and salt and pepper.

3. Lay a slice of cucumber on the plate you will serve the appetizer on. Add a heaping tablespoon of the chicken salad on the cucumber, lay another piece on top.

4. Use toothpick to hold it together. Place Kalamata, black or green olives through the top of the toothpick to pretty it up!

5. Keep refrigerated until ready to serve. Enjoy.

# Ham and Dill Pickle Bites

Total time: 50 minutes

Preparation time: 5 minutes

Cooking time: 45 minutes

**Cooking Ingredients:**

- Dill pickles
- Thin deli ham slices
- Cream cheese (or use whipped cream cheese if you prefer)

**Cooking Instructions:**

1. Let the cream cheese sit for at least 30 minutes at room temperature before you make these.

2. Cut dill pickles lengthwise into sixths, depending on how thick the pickles are. You need as many cut pickle spears as you have ham slices.

3. Spread each slice of ham with a very thin layer of cream cheese. Place a dill pickle on the edge of each ham slice.

4. Then roll up the ham around the dill pickle, and place toothpicks where you want each piece to be cut.

5. Arrange on plate and serve. Enjoy.

# Cheesy Spicy Sausage Stuffed Mushrooms

Preparation time: 20 minutes

Cooking time: 30 minutes

Total time 50 minutes

Servings: 12 People

Calories: 164 kcal

## Cooking Ingredients:

- 24 ounces Baby Bella mushrooms stems removed
- 12 ounces of pork sausage
- 1 teaspoon garlic powder
- 1 teaspoon dried basil
- 1 teaspoon dried parsley
- 2 to 3 teaspoons chili pepper
- 8 ounces of cream cheese softened
- Optional: Gourmet Garden Slightly Dried Chili Pepper Flakes and Parsley
- Get Ingredients Powered by Chicory

## Cooking Instructions:

1. Start by heating the oven to 350 degrees F. Then scoop the inside of each mushroom to make room for the stuffing.

2. Add each mushroom into a 9 by 13 baking dish. In a skillet over medium heat, brown the sausage.

3. Once browned add stir in pastes and stir to combine. Taste and adjust seasonings to your taste.

4. Place the cream cheese in a stand mixer then add in your sausage. Blend until fully mixed.

5. Stuff each mushroom with mixture. Bake for about 25 to 30 minutes.

6. Remove from oven, sprinkle on chili pepper and parsley if desired.

7. Remove mushrooms to a serving platter. Enjoy.

# Buffalo Cauliflower Bites with Dairy Free Ranch Dressing

Preparation time: 15 minutes

Cooking time: 30 minutes

Total time: 45 minutes

Servings: 8 Serves

Calories: 268 kcal

## Cooking Ingredients:

- 4 cups of cauliflower florets
- 2 tablespoons of extra virgin olive oil
- ¼ teaspoon of salt
- ¼ teaspoon of smoked paprika
- ¼ teaspoon of garlic powder
- ½ cup of sugar free hot sauce I used Archie Moore's brand
- Dairy Free Ranch Dressing
- 1 cup organic mayonnaise
- ½ cup of Silk unsweetened coconut milk
- 1 teaspoon of garlic powder
- 1 teaspoon of onion powder
- ¼ teaspoon of pepper
- 1 tablespoon of fresh lemon juice
- ¼ cup fresh chopped parsley
- Get Ingredients Powered by Chicory

## Cooking Instructions:

1. First heat oven to 400 degrees F. Spray baking sheet with non-stick olive oil cooking spray.

2. Place florets in a large bowl and toss with olive oil. In a small bowl mix the salt, paprika and garlic powder together with hot sauce.

3. Add the hot sauce into cauliflower bowl and stir well until well coated. Spread cauliflower out evenly on baking sheet and bake for 30 minutes.

4. Whisk ingredients together and pour into a mason jar. Cover and refrigerate until ready to serve with cauli bites.

# Mini Zucchini Pizza Bites

Preparation time: 15 minutes

Cooking time: 15 minutes

Total time: 30 minutes

Servings: 6

Calories: 230 kcal

**Cooking Ingredients:**

- 2 cups shredded zucchini
- 1 egg
- 1 teaspoon of Italian Seasonings
- ½ teaspoon of salt
- ¼ teaspoon of pepper
- ½ cup of grated provolone cheese
- 1 cup shredded mozzarella cheese
- ¼ cup of mini pepperoni slices
- Get Ingredients Powered by Chicory

**Cooking Instructions:**

1. First heat oven to 400 degrees. Grease a mini muffin pan with natural olive oil cooking spray.

2. Place the zucchini in a clean towel and squeeze as much liquid out as you can. Mix the zucchini, egg, Italian seasoning, salt, pepper and provolone cheese and cilantro in a bowl.

3. Equally divide the mixture into the mini muffin pan, packed down in each cup. Then sprinkle mozzarella onto zucchini then top with mini pepperoni slices.

4. Bake for about 15 to 18 minutes until golden brown around the edges.

5. Allow to cool about 10 minutes before removing. Let cool.

6. Use a knife to cut around edges to loosen from muffin pan.

7. Serve and enjoy.

# Sugar Free Sweet & Spicy Bacon Chicken Bites

Preparation time: 20 minutes

Cooking time: 30 minutes

Total time 50 minutes

Servings: 8 people

**Cooking Ingredients:**

- 2 pounds of chicken tenderloin boneless, cut into 1 inch cubes
- 16 ounces of bacon cut into fourths (I used Applegate)
- ½ cup of Swerve sweetener
- 1 teaspoon of chili powder
- ½ teaspoon of pepper
- Get Ingredients Powered by Chicory

**Cooking Instructions:**

1. First heat oven to 400 degrees F and then wrap the bacon over each piece of chicken.

2. Prepare two baking sheets with aluminium foil or you can use a cooling rack over the baking pan.

3. In a bowl whisk the last 3 ingredients together and roll each chicken bite into the mixture.

4. Place chicken bites on baking pans or cooling rack over pans and bake for about 25 to 30 minutes.

5. Serve immediately. Enjoy.

# Baked Cream Cheese Crab Dip

Preparation time: 5 minutes

Cooking time: 30 minutes

Total time: 35 minutes

Servings: 12 people

Calories: 142kcal

**Cooking Ingredients:**

- 8 oz. lump crab meat
- 8 oz. cream cheese softened
- ½ cup avocado mayonnaise
- 1 tablespoon lemon juice
- 1 teaspoon Worcestershire sauce
- ½ teaspoon of garlic powder
- ½ teaspoon of onion powder
- ½ teaspoon of salt
- ¼ teaspoon of dry mustard
- ¼ teaspoon of black pepper

**Cooking Instructions:**

1. Add all ingredients into small baking dish and spread out evenly. Bake at 375°F for about 25 to 30 minutes.

2. Serve with low carb crackers or vegetables. Enjoy.

# Philly Cheesesteak Stuffed Mushrooms

Preparation time: 15 minutes

Cooking time: 15 minutes

Total time: 30 minutes

## Cooking Ingredients:

- 24 oz. baby bella mushrooms
- 1 cup chopped red pepper
- 1 cup chopped onion
- 2 tablespoons butter
- 1 teaspoon salt divided
- ½ teaspoon of pepper divided
- 1 pound of beef sirloin shaved or thinly sliced against the grain
- 4 ounces of provolone cheese
- Get Ingredients Powered by Chicory

## Cooking Instructions:

1. First heat oven to 350 degrees. Remove stems from mushrooms and place mushrooms on a greased baby sheet.

2. Sprinkle with ½ teaspoon of salt and ¼ teaspoon of pepper on both sides and bake for 15 minutes. Set aside.

3. Melt 1 tablespoon butter in a large skillet and cook pepper and onions until soft. Then season with ½ teaspoon of salt and ¼ teaspoon of pepper.

4. Remove from the skillet and set aside. In the same skillet, melt the remaining tablespoon of butter and cook the meat to your preference.

5. Add the provolone cheese and stir until completely melted. Return back the veggies.

6. Add mixture into the mushrooms, top with more cheese if you like and bake for 5 minutes.

7. Serve and enjoy.

# Cheddar Cheese Straws and the Cabot Fit Team

Serves: 24 straws

Preparation time: 5 minutes

Cooking time: 35 minutes

Total time: 40 minutes

**Cooking Ingredients:**

- 1 & ¼ cup of almond flour
- 2 tablespoons of coconut flour I used Bob's Red Mill
- 2 tablespoon of arrowroot starch I used Bob's Red Mill
- 1 teaspoon of xanthan gum
- ½ teaspoon of garlic powder
- ¼ teaspoon of salt
- 5 tablespoons of butter well chilled and cut into small pieces
- 2 to 4 tablespoons of ice water
- 4 ounces of finely shredded sharp cheddar

**Cooking Instructions:**

1. Combine almond flour, coconut flour, arrowroot starch, xanthan gum, garlic powder and salt in the bowl of a food processor. Pulse a few times to mix.

2. Evenly sprinkle butter over almond flour mixture and pulse until it resembles fine crumbs.

3. Add water through feeding tube 1 tablespoon at a time until dough clumps together (Turn processor to low).

4. Form into a flat disc and cover with plastic wrap. Chill 30 minutes. Meanwhile preheat oven to 300F and line a large baking sheet with parchment paper.

5. Take about 1 tablespoon of dough and roll it between your palms. Continue to roll gently on a piece of parchment.

6. Sprinkle evenly a few teaspoons of grated cheddar and gently press the cheese into the stick to adhere. Transfer to prepared baking sheet.

7. Do the same for remaining dough and cheese. Bake for 25 to 30 minutes, until firm and cheese is lightly browned.

8. Remove from oven and let cool completely. Enjoy.

# Crispy Parmesan Tomato Chips

Servings: 6 People

Preparation time: 10 minutes

Cooking time: 5 hours

Total time: 5 hours 10 minutes

Calories: 88 kcal

## Cooking Ingredients:

- 6 cups thinly sliced beefsteak tomatoes
- 2 tablespoons extra virgin olive oil
- 2 tsp. sea salt
- 1 tsp. garlic powder
- 2 tablespoons fresh chopped parsley
- 2 tablespoons grated Parmesan cheese

## Cooking Instructions:

1. Gently drizzle and toss the sliced tomatoes in the olive oil to coat slices and place slices without overlapping in a baking pan.

2. Preheat oven to 200 degrees F. Combine and whisk the remaining ingredients together in a small bowl whisk.

3. Sprinkle mixture over each slice. Depending on how thick the slices of tomato are check every 30 minutes until edges show some charring, could take 4 to 5 hours.

4. Serve and enjoy.

# Smoked Salmon & Cucumber

Preparation time: 5 minutes

Cooking time: 15 minutes

Gross time: 20 minutes

Servings: 24 Servings

Calories: 20.7kcal

## Cooking Ingredients:

- ½ cup non-fat plain Greek yogurt
- 1 tablespoon capers chopped
- 1 tablespoon chopped dill
- 24 ¼ -inch thick English cucumber slices
- 4 ounces smoked salmon cut into 24 pieces
- Dill for garnish


## Cooking Instructions:

1. Mix together the Greek yogurt, capers and chopped dill in a small bowl.

2. Place 1 teaspoon of yogurt sauce onto each cucumber slice.

3. Then top each with a piece of smoked salmon and a small sprig of dill.

4. Serve and enjoy.

# Acknowledgement

In preparing the "**The Keto Diet Cookbook for Beginners**", I sincerely wish to acknowledge my indebtedness to my husband for his support and the wholehearted cooperation and vast experience of my two colleagues - Mrs. Alexandra Bryne, and Mrs. Catherine Long.

**BABARA SAULS**

Lightning Source UK Ltd.
Milton Keynes UK
UKHW050634290421
382833UK00008B/246